This book is dedicated to:

First and foremost to my mother, as I doubt I ever could have been able to complete the amount of internal work I have so far without her love and support.

Friends and family, I could fill up the pages of a book with your names and thanks alone, for brevity's sake you are here.

Lovers who have hurt me, honestly I feel like a large portion of this book wouldn't exist if it weren't for my over-sensitivity. Thanks for the cool lines and lessons. I still love you through distance and time but in a healthy way.

Anyone who reads this book and connects with some element within. If you can relate to what I share, we are united in our suffering and hope.

Anyone who reads this book and connects with nothing in it. I couldn't exist in the fluffy world of the universal yes. Your disinterest in what I share gives it so much more meaning to myself and those who connect with it. Your validation isn't necessary for my existence or to enjoy sharing my experience.

My future lover whose absence has allowed me space to grow as an individual and figure out what being a man is and isn't about. Even without meeting you formally yet, I know you are a formidable force of awesomeness who will rock my existence at its foundation. You even get your own poem at the end of the book.

Finally, the Tao, the Mysteries, the Way, whatever you want to call it. Thank you for all the situations, pain, happiness, ecstasy and misery that was necessary to write this book and give me such a varied life. Looking back I see your watermark on the whole process. You are a funny trickster.

About the Author:

I'm too insane to explain and you're too "normal" to understand.
- Anonymous

My story is on the cover, what follows is just the translation and
dialogue.

My soul is on paper
If you wish to see
All you need to do
Is read

If you read these words
An opinion of me will form
Even if you have never met me
Be wise and realize I am releasing
What I have already absorbed
This life, its flavor and texture
I am neither crazy nor sane
Just alive, adapting, and witnessing

Not all these words were lived
Some are mere images staining my brain
Cheesy B movie cut scenes
They are just verbal diarrhea
Expelling the sickness
That plagues my empty soul

My soul was broken and emptied
Only to be filled with what it was searching for
I say
The quest that caused it to break and empty
Was successful by its failure

By reading this you choose to embark on a fool's journey as a witness
You will read the suffering and hope of a madman
You will see through the eyes of a poetic romantic drug addict
As well as through the eyes of a recovering soul
Intent on establishing some semblance of sanity
Be cautious reader, you are treading through my past
Through my heart, mind and soul.

The cover was illustrated by Sharaya Anastasiya an artist / illustrator, residing in BC, Canada. Sharaya is well versed in illustrating the weird and the wonderful.

———

If you would like to learn more about Ross' journey visit his website www.thespiritualphoenix.com

For items intent on aiding you in furthering your journey inward visit www.thespiritualphoenix.com/shop

You can also listen to Ross' two podcasts: The Spiritual Phoenix Podcast and Phoenix Poetry Podcast available on Itunes, Google Play, Soundcloud and more.

If you enjoy this book you can expect some other work from Ross in the future. Here are some other projects he has percolating with no set date for completion or release.

An autobiography
A self-help system using imagination, creativity and magic
A psychedelic spirituality fantasy novel
A gonzo style psychedelic sci-fi memoir
A daily meditation book
And a few other tricks up his sleeve

If you enjoy reading Vagrant Verses please leave an honest review on your purchasing platform and share it with a friend.

If you would like to contact Ross directly please email him at Ross@thespiritualphoenix.com

Vagrant Verses

Poems of Madness, Disease, and Hope

Written By Ross Cessna
Cover Art by Sharaya Anastasiya

Poems of a Vagabond

These poems come from a time of shifting landscapes in my physical, mental and spiritual life. They were composed from the middle of August 2008 until around the middle of December 2008. During this time I was homeless for a month. I traveled from Sultan Washington, to Arcata California, where I alternated between being homeless sleeping on the beach, in baseball fields and seedy motels. The next leg of my journey led me back to Las Vegas after leaving the area in June of the same year. Two weeks in Vegas led me back to Ohio. A month or so in Ohio led me back to Vegas for about another month. This was a beautifully trying time and although some of the poems from this portion of my life succumbed to flames in the grips of psychosis that would come later, I believe you are being presented with what you are supposed to see from that time. I pay homage to the pages that I returned to the mysteries.

August 2008 - December 2008

August 24th

Please rain cleanse my sins
Wash this dirt
So I can be clean again
Watch my hurt
That I cover with grins
Seep into my skin
And cleanse within

August 25th

Free range tactics
To escape the plastic
Yeah it's a struggle
Snap back like elastic
Know you like the style
Cuz you can't match it

August 31st

I can hear the trees talking
As they bang together
Moved by the wind
They whisper the word freedom
A blue patch of sky
One bird soaring
Is the only opening in the canopy
Freedom

Sept 2nd

Slept on the beach
Right next to the ocean
Wishin and hopin
I get my groove in motion

October 5th

Every night I dream of you
But you're never by my side
I lost you and I know it's true
Cuz of what eats me inside
My worlds cracking and crumbling
And tears fill up my eyes
My hearts drunk and stumbling
But I'm left wondering why
You are the only lady
That I will ever need
But every time I pull you close
I show insecurities

Oct 6th

A victim of the system
Won't be whipped to submission

I wonder why I wander
My life made to ponder
Got no destination
But for how much longer
Wish my soul was stronger
But my mind is on her

A lost soul in this life
Stumbling under street lights
Wondering what is right
Got my blood and this life
Got some love and this light
Got no one but I'm right

Take your government
I don't want none of it
Got my vice
And I'm loving it
Another glutton for punishment
Not afraid
Won't run from it
A runaway loving it

If you wanna dissect me
Come at it correctly
Another lost soul
Who won't sign a check b
Another broken soul
Who's trying to fill his holes
Another lost cause
With no control
Another last place
Who won't make pole

Just another late night
No fist fights
But no highlights
Another escape from limelight
Sighs under twilight

I'm just trying to escape
But I got no glass to break
Like I'm stuck in second place
A body with no face
Always in last place

It's one
Ain't got friends
Got no bills to lend
Not one to pretend
A story with an end
Gotta find a way to escape this
Since I was born trying to erase it
Can't find a way to face it
24 years old and I ain't made shit

Just want one more drink
Before I walk away
Too many drinks
And too many words to say
But I got no one to talk to
Got no one to listen
Just got these verbs
And my mic in position

Warm sun on a cold heart
Beat up sneakers on broken glass
Strong soul struggling to survive
Morning at a Vegas bus stop

Escapism or self-exploration
Self-destructive or tough love
Runaway or wanderer
Victim or target

Broken tired faces
The smell of sweat and body odor
Ahh the bus

The wheels spin on hot asphalt
Another run over
And stuck face first in tar
The hunger of the machine

Scratched glass
With gang logos
Seats reupholstered
With gum corpses

Dusty rust spots
From desert pilgrimage
Leaving heaven
To enter hell

The taste of Budweiser
Ahh American piss water
Trying to escape in the
Redneck holy water

Broken shattered heart
Crystallized nightmares
Replaying again
On late night TV

Do you know the place where angels fuck?
Have you seen the source of starvation?
Do you know how lies taste after continuous service?
Have you seen the man who invented war?

Cracked asphalt and broken wine bottles
Another universe, stars twinkling in lamplight
Oil spots collect and absorb the light, only black
The gravel chunks float in an unknown ether

I dream in colors
I live in wonder
I breathe deeply
I move slowly

I have been ill from truth
I have been sick from lies
I have been awake for nightmares
I have been asleep through dreams

Straw hat and liver spots
Hatchet wound in leather
With 3 teeth and cheap wine breath
2 shopping carts and 10 dollars

Do I know you from somewhere?
Another life perhaps?
Have you seen
Other souls before

                              Have you wandered
                    Where dreams go when they die
                        I would like to find mine
                           And pay my respects

I found heaven one day
I found hell later that evening

                         Cheap wine and cigarettes
                                Guitar and books
                           Solitude and sanctuary
                           My life and my prison

I
Am
The
Only
Rebel
Seeing
Failing
Mindsets
TIDALWAVE

                           I see your lip quivering
                       But you just ain't giving in
                     All these sins you're swimming in
                          Got you up to the neck

Eat your psychedelics to touch god
Chemically induced spirituality
Psilocybin induced religion
Edible natural mystic

Been chasing your dream
The rest falls in between
Starts trickling downstream
To fill in the cracks
Your heart is broken pieces
Jumbled words
Without a thesis
To fill the gaps

I've tasted lies like yours before
My mouth is still raw and full of sores

Hello my name is Time
I consume everything
Even myself

Street light halos
On a cold desert night
Their light, cool, metallic
As we navigate, the artificial jungle (junkie)

Religion is fiction
Secondhand interpretations of non-existent situations
Spirituality is seeing
Whether in nature
Or chemically induced states

Her tears were cooked up heroin
She caught them in a needle
As they rolled from her face
Just to reinject them into her veins

Eat your psychedelics to escape
Hopefully your mind is cozy
Dark things under the surface
Could appear in hallucinations

                                                    Can I say I hate you
                                                And your cold hard shapes
                                                      I used to love you
                                              And your soft warm symbols

Can I fuck the stars?
I came quick
She was faking it
The birth of a new universe

                                              Some are the thought police
                                            Something in your mind unsaid
                                                    Are fights or questions
                                             Just let me think how I will

I sold my soul to a pawn shop
Twelve dollars and fifty cents!
Hopefully they don't realize it's broken
Till I get out the door

                                        6 month escape plan to California
                                                  Avoid the law, no court!
                                                 Save money, the struggle
                                               Stay on point, the problem

Broken dreams for sale
Buy, sell or trade
Buy 1 get 1 free
Now accepting applications

                                                   I dream of barbed wire
                                                            Frozen in ice
                                               I dream of children's toys
                                                             Left in shit
                                            Where are the happy dreams?
                                                   Ones lost to childhood
                                                   Bright smiling faces
                                                   And talking squirrels

If you read these words
An opinion of me will form
Even if you have never met me
Be wise and realize I am releasing
What I have already absorbed
This life, its flavor and texture
I am neither crazy nor sane
Just alive, adapting, and witnessing

I am an over indulger
If I like something
I want it constantly
I struggle to dislike more things

She was high on oxycodone
When she cut herself
She drank her blood
To keep the buzz going

Cool blue sky
Birds talking in tongues
Sunlight through leaves and branches
A rebirth to life

I have always been a deep kid
I remember 6 or 7
Walking on an iced over creek
Mom and Dad still married on Silica road
Thinking about how I didn't want to die
I figured it was cold when you died
And you floated alone in the black sky
Forever

I remember ergot induced
Macaroni movement at the dinner table
I had black veins
Needed a diamond shower

The silence of sleep
The stillness of death
The breathing of meditation
Replenished spiritual energy

                              I lack an enemy beyond myself
                              Almost everyone likes me but me
                                        Why do I hate myself?
                              Shifty eyes and no direction.

Cuts and bruises on high cheekbones
Cocaine mixed with blood encrusted nostrils
Blacked out in a crack house
Giving hand jobs for cigarettes
Giving head to feed her kids
Fucking to pay her rent
The angels cry and demons smile
Over the lost souls seizuring from stress

                                   Her mouth salivates semen
                              It hangs in elastic bands down her lips
                              Smeared mascara and cheap perfume
                                   You don't kiss a hooker.

I have seen things
More beautiful than you can imagine
With my own two eyes
Nature
I have seen things
More warped than you can fathom
In nighttime subconscious thought
Nightmares

                              I want a girl with crazy eyes
                                        Who cries LSD
                              Who kisses me with shotguns
                                   Who lives to wander

Will you ever see the sunrise
Exactly on the opposite side of the world
From where you stand today

                    Love is a luxury item
             When shared beyond family
                 It's something you want
             Not something you NEED

Not all these words were lived
Some are mere images staining my brain
Cheesy B movie cut scenes
They are just verbal diarrhea
Expelling the sickness
That plagues my empty soul

           As I write these words, I send love
           My love to you as warm as can be
             I think of you, thinking of me
               Warm, addictive, love

Do you use your brain?
Intelligence squandered
On constant internal investigations
Making a larger void

                    She bit her lip
               Warm red dribbles
                 Crimson tears
        I kissed her and tasted her essence

Thumb tacks in eyes
He doesn't want to see any more
Late night TV news or reality shows
He wants blind deaf solitude

                I remember happiness
                It makes you weak
      Sadness is a like a cold day without a jacket
           At first you feel it then you adapt
            Happiness is an addiction
        You gotta have a fix all the time
      Only thing is there aren't many dealers
         For something you can't sell

Why do I wish non-existence?
Nothing would matter
I would return to the energy
Of the universe

She likes / hates me
She wants me / another
I love / hate her
I want her / death

Tiny crystallized teardrops
Turning to acid and scarring his face
Stinging his tired soul
Saying "What's up, fucker!?"

Bed eyed and half awake
Smoking a cigarette
Contemplating heavy thoughts
At 8:30 am

Lies
Carefully constructed deception
How many lives does she live?
I will never know

Simplification
1 good woman
To grow old with
And keep him in line

Hello little bird
Bopping on rocks
Eating flower seeds
Flying to the pomegranate tree

I don't write poems
In THIS book for others
These are for me
A healthy purge

Where are our minds?
Aisle 7, next to People magazine.

Happiness is constructed
Framed by wants and needs
If built with less wants
You also have less needs

An old Indian
Living alone in desert mountains
Red sun, on leathery red skin, on red rocks
Unaware of the outside world
He doesn't know cities or money
He doesn't know George Bush or Obama
He knows LIFE

Spontaneous combustion
The ultimate escape
Or
Premature understanding (enlightenment)

X-Ray glasses
And time machines
Truth serum
And mind control
UFOs
And other realms

Your soft breathing while you sleep
Angelic dreaming face
Your eyes with tender sympathy
Melting my heart

Constructing constellations
That spell I love you
So not a night passes
Where you don't know

Counting the minutes
Away from you
Makes seeing you again
That much sweeter

I love you
I love me
I love us
I love life

                    I burned your love letter
                    The words were ash
                    Before I lit them anyhow
                    Light crumbling dust

Cold wet
Grey
Unseen Horizon
My life or the city

                    The warm love he felt
                    That kept him strong
                    Has faded
                    To hurt, and hate. Rejection

By the time you want me again
My heart will be dead and cold
Funny how the thing you wanted last year
Has become a burden today

                    Wish I knew the words
                    To tell myself
                    You are poison. A spiritual vampire
                    But I remain mute

I can choose to be sad
Till I overcome it
Or hate
To expedite the process

                    I wanna lay face first
                    in stagnant black water
                    Choked with mud and shit
                    To fill my lungs

I see the most beautiful things
I see the ugliest things
Duality of existence
At its finest.

I want you to love me
Or leave
Don't wanna be dragged
Behind your doomed voyage

My tears are cold
Dry puffs of dust
I lay shriveled and dehydrated
From my purge

I walked along black rivers
In the gray mist of the city
Getting rained on
It made my day better
Tears are socially unacceptable
No one wants depressed friends
They want happy shiny faces
To maintain their balance

Rain thanks for cleansing me
Tiny silver sin shower

Grey days make me smile
Looking at black water
Choking the gutters
Looking at pine cones to race

I find happiness in strange places
I did meditative purging walking in the grey
The transient points to happiness
You need grey days to purge depression with rain
And the hope for sunshine too
Following grey clouds
Sometimes it takes longer
But that's life

                                             Got to move on
                                          To save my love inside
                                           Can't be your friend
                                           We gotta say goodbye

I shut down all your feelings
Emotional terrorist dealings
But I was dead inside
And now my soul's alive

                        I give myself one more year to settle down with a girl
                                   I think after that all is said and done
                                        I will become a world traveler
                                      Writing visions, poems, journals

Another night
Past life reflections
Mirror of before
Same exact place

                                             Pessimistic piss-ant
                                           Affordable amiability
                                                 Self-conscious
                                           Self-fulfilling prophecy

I dream of soft
Warm love
Or cold dark
Travel places

                                               So many chumps
                                              Punk ass bitches
                                              Fake but living
                              Chasing and damaging the realness

Why do I sit at bars?
Writing, thinking
All others here
Shutting off thought

                                        Stoic tragedies
                             And metaphysical anomalies
                                     Navigate cold streets
                                   Late night choked with fog

I have lived
Cold hearted heart throbs
And through warm love
Feeling ice cold

                                   I dream unaltered shapes
                                       Vision and prophecy
                                       Tragic dreamscapes
                                       Poisoned by reality

Hopes to reach the bridge
Attest happy visions
To vixens who live
Across the bar

                                   Tender chicken scratch
                                       Vivacious verbiage
                                   Is permeating my ozone
                             Fucking up my homeostasis

Star crossed lover eyes
Side glancing when gazes meet
Is it fear?
Or just icy avoidance of love?

                                   Angel's cold hard realities
                       Rehashed over sentimental situations
                                   Poisoned consciousness
                                       Altering mindsets

I dream warm vague
Shapes, sizes and forms

Stone cold sophistication
Last minute lust
Pessimistic purity
Soiled soul

                                        Words transcribe no more than present
                                                    Future is prophesied
                                            All other words spoken
                                            Remain past reflections

Love lost principles
Extracted in oval
Tantric shapes
Poison.

                                                    Horrific visages
                                                    Satanic scribbles
                                            Lime light cigarettes
                                                    Potential poison

No sophomorish reflexes
Only senioresque emptiness
DJs that dismantle
Reality

                                                    I caught the girl
                                                    Across the way
                                                    Giving me
                                            Exposed eyes!!!

Pen and pencil twitch
Loose emotions
All alone
No emotions

                                            Lady I don't want
                                            Dream fed reality
                                            Don't promise both
                                            Heaven and hell

I inject optimism
Intravenously
Hard to quit
Deep addictions

Potential possibilities plundered
Enjoy
Self-exclusion and cynicism
Cold words reheated

Lost conversations
To the lovely lady
Across the bar
Wearing turquoise

O.D.B. (Old dirty bastard)
Cross glances
You got what I need
Crystallized emotion

I dream in color
I love fully
Open hearted
Reckless loving

She touches places in me
Places I thought dead
She moves my world
Crazy love

Wish I could stop
Loving her so much
Wish I could
Change the past

I roam
Cold black asphalt
Cracked concrete
Dark lit roads and alleys
Searching through
The filth of the city
Looking for a treasure
To soothe my soul

Pen pushing wizards
Writing world plans
Consumer conscious devils
Digging ditches covertly

She's a gypsy princess
Searching for herself
Singing for her escape
Into emotional health
White angel wings
Holding the world on its axis

Every circumstance happens for a reason
Love or rejection
Happiness or sadness
It's all preparation

Tired sleep filled eyes
Strained vertebrates
5 o'clock shadow
And hand rolled cigarettes

Lost orange balloon
Floating away in desert blue
Going on its own path
Leaving all others behind

Methamphetamine mistress
Shook up and cooked up
Vicodin vampires
Shutting down souls

Living life on cracked concrete
Only sound pavement and feet

Sugar coated insensitivity
Served by a dead heart
For self-preservation
And emotional damnation

He looks at the world
Through hungover eyes
All he sees
Is plastic tragedies

Broken beauties
With synthetic tears
Socially shutdown
Lacking sophistication

I see tragic shapes
Painted on billboards
Societies formed
By consumer Ideals

Bleak and brainwashed
Happiness through objects
Filling the void
With possessions
Temporary tourniquets
To stop social bleeding

Lonely dove
Sitting on a telephone wire
Another shade of grey
Melting into the clouds

The birds on the lighted tower
Sit like Greek Gods
On Mt. Olympus
Looking down on their subjects

Shutting down love
For a soul who wants none
It is her loss
I could give her the stars

Cold stiff fingers
Flexing to feel warm
On skyless
Grey days over taking

Autumn colored leaves
On a pomegranate tree
Fat fruits hang from branches like Christmas decorations
December in the desert

Bird landing on the lamppost
Walking through the flowers
Hopping along on rocks only to fly away
How I wish I lived your life

The only way to never lose
Is to never possess
By not having anything
You never lose anything

I shiver from the cold
Cold and stiff flesh
The living dead
But torture is freeing

He dreams of broken glass
Shattered pieces of the past
Internal hallucinations
Of a tortured imagination

Don't tell me your dreams
Save them for yourself
Others may not like yours
Best to indulge in that privately

I hope to walk away
From this touch and go
Game in a twisted funhouse
Of emotional pain and suffering

                              GOODBYE Love in my heart
                               No chance to feel for her
                                   Lost and shut down
                                       Sliding away
                                    Gone into the gray

Clouds, dark purple
Rise like smoke over mountains
Streaks of blue
Breaking through fiery orange, Clouds

                              Mountains, purple in sunset
                              With orange and purple, clouds
                                  Streaking above them
                              Only to fade into cold blue

The dying sunset
Looking like cold embers
Burning out an arctic fire
To make the heavens dark and cold

                                 The orange has faded
                                  Heaven is burning
                                 And the smoke blows
                                 The winds of change

Heaven is burning
Thick dark tentacles reach to it
Jagged purple teeth bite at it
The day has ended.

                                                    Your name is bitter to speak
                                                    It makes my eyes water
                                                    And choke on the air
                                                    Gagging at the utterance

Enjoy
Searching for love
On cold moonless nights
Late at night, dead inside
All you want is a smile
Someone who understands
Someone who listens
Someone who turned you away

                                                    Damn her
                                                    Freshly erased from thought
                                                    The voice of the angels
                                                    Reopen unhealed wounds

I want a beautiful face
Filled with love and kisses
Eyes for me
And an unavailable heart

                                                    My mind aches
                                                    Thinking of past and future
                                                    My mind aches
                                                    Thinking of the present

You freeze souls
With artic words
Glaciers flow
Out of your heart

                                                    The creation of words
                                                    The destruction of society
                                                    The start of classification
                                                    The end of anonymity

                                           Dazed
                          He stares out the window
                                        Watching
                          The world pass him by

I bend words
You break hearts
I build ideas
You shatter dreams

                                   What do you live for?
                                  What would you die for?
                         Could they make a movie of your life?
                                     Would people watch?

When you look at me
What do you see?
Self-destructive tendencies
Or a social rebel

                              Your words are bitter sweet
                              Sugar coated words of love
                                       Help to conceal
                              The bitter taste of rejection

Your words
Cold reheated
Hypocrisies
½ off

                                       I know you bleed
                                          I know you cry
                                       I know you love
                                       But why not me

I sit looking at a car
What is her name?
Who does she love?
What is her life?

Late night
And lonely
I envy homeless couples
Even those with nothing have more than me

Why do you call me?
Why do you care?
Let me slip away
My services are not needed

I cry for love
Like an addict
I crave
Junk starved cells

What will you do
With your words
Build empires
Or shatter hopes

The taste of broken dreams
Halitosis and cellophane
Stale cigarettes and cheap beer
Stick to your mouth

People sit here drinking socially
To forget
I sit here writing
Examining internal landscapes

Words, words, words
That is all I write
Trying to elaborate
On the void

Do these words sting?
Do they pull at your heart?
Do you judge?
Or do you understand

I see smiling faces
They make me smile
Falsification
Of my own hell

Pen caresses paper
Like virgin lovers
Uneducated
But passionately

Touch my soul
Be someone different
Not these abominations
Of A Brave New World

I see every lady look at me
{EGO} I am a rarity
Aware of the world
For what it is / isn't

Empty beer bottles
Sucking out suds
Surrounded by beautiful people
Whose ½ full cup is waste

I know what you want
Hope, peace, dreams
They are all sold
Into prostitution

Happy couples
Make single souls ache
Where is my bookend
Who will help balance the weight I hold

Am I escaping
Or formulating a plan
You sit running
I sit scheming

All these carbon copy
Cookie cutter
Dust ruffle
Souls

I dream of softness
Warm happy hearts
I live a life of hardships
Cold sad soul

I see you
Brawn, strength
Raw, rough
Muscle
I function
Verbally
Do you wish to battle
Pen vs. sword

My soul is on paper
If you wish to see
All you need to do
Is read

Psychedelic religions
Formed from hallucinations
I pray by your side
For the soul of humanity

Only through deep
Rigorous contemplation
And action
Can salvation be reached

Run from your dreams
Chase your nightmares
Lean into the sharp points
They are duller than you think

I hear the same
Conversation
The words are different
Still similar
Nothing, Nothing, Nothing
"I am a cog"
I function
Without thought

Fade away
You give me no comfort
You want what I have
But don't want the ticket

I see your smoking heels
Why do you run?
Where are you going?
Do you even know?

I see your fakeness
You try to hide it
But it bleeds through
A vibrant crimson
Staining your holy robes
You walk by oblivious
As if to discredit
All those who see

You want friendship
I want love
No one wins
Why do you try?

When I stop writing
I die
Whether figuratively
Or physically

Try to understand
I am not bitter
I just don't share your vision
Can't see what is not there

Take your calloused heart
I have no time to peel
All the layers
You have built up

Why does God laugh
At all my attempts
I feel like a favorite
A regular, on God's comedy channel

What have you burned
Love? Hope? Trust?
I have scorched all
I walk in the ashes

How many people laugh
At the loner
Writing out his thoughts
Pussy

I am selfish I guess
I want someone to love
Someone to smile
At me for me

I see silent loners
Lost in thought
Staring into space
Ahh the tortured

I see happy couples
They magnify my loneliness
Unoriginal reprints
Consuming the gorgeous

I hang upside down
Attached to a dirtball
Floating through space
Supported by theories

What do you want?
I don't got it
I have nothing
And want less

Black and white
American bhikkhus
Living in celluloid
Stereotyped

How many pages?
How many words?
How many letters?
Will pour from my pen

I've seen your kind
Living for the future
Stepping over puddles
Keeping white shoes outta the mud

Pray to your god
In a house built of sin
How aware are you
Of cosmic karma baggage

What do you see?
Words?
Thoughts?
Insanity?
I see purity
Nothing is unspeakable
Only some are incapable

Do I run?
No, I only stumble
Do I climb?
No, I only fall
Do I strive?
No, I only attempt
Do I live?
Yes, full and rich

Don't try to think
Only exist
Now.
All else is fruitless

Vivacious verbiage
Venting vicious vendettas
Worthless words
Wither worlds whole

I write four line thoughts
Sometimes less or more
So they are digestible
Objections to reality

I look in the mirror
Tired damaged eyes
With wild tendencies
Sedated by addictions

I see so much
Words fall short
Hard to describe
Life in a sentence

Just once
Can't I find a lady
Far beyond my league
Recovering in the minors

Lines, curves and bends
That is what you read
Your programming makes you see
Words, thoughts, ideas

How many ladies
Dream of poets
Unaware
One sits here

If you died now
What would be your last
Words? Thoughts? Prayers?
Think about it.
NOW!

I see sloppy fucks
With beautiful women
The power of money
Makes slobs attractive

I would rather be penniless
And have ugly love
Than rich
With beautiful surrender

Can you put a price
On love, attraction, dreams
For some
All is for sale

All these ladies want
Is bullshit
Sit on a soap box
Selling placebos

How many more thoughts
Will pulse
Through my fractured
Hopeless mind

Why do I sit
Lonely
So many people
Looking for friends

How many faces
Places, new spaces
Will pass over
My burned out retinas

I see smiles
I taste dreams
I feel pain
I smell death

Beautiful girl
With a hundred dollar bill
Why does she pine
For who she is with

What does he have that I don't
Bullshit!!
He has lies
For sale

Words are bitter
Thoughts are cheap
Minds are cheap
Hopes are cheap

Hello parallel
Dreams
Schemes, seams
What are your names?

         I taste blood
       Iron rich iconoclasts
        I dream colors
      Acid rich aristocracies

Bleed, Bleed, Bleed
Dream, Dream, Dream
Scheme, Scheme, Scheme
What is as it seems?

       Curly haired deficiencies
      Straight haired thoughtlessness
       Dream broken efficiencies
        Love broken marriages

Why do I sit here
Dreaming
When do I stop
These nightmares

         Taste colors
         See sounds
        Feel thoughts
          Live life

Black and white blondes
Living
Celluloid fantasies
Trapped in the past

I see your eyes
Dreaming, scheming
Looking for late night
Loving or heartbreak

Watcha want lovely
Rich fantasies
Or do you chase
Poor realities

Dream of escape
Pray for reality
Accept existence
Worship worldliness

Who loves this?
Me? You? Yours?
I say burn
Hopes and dreams

It's 12:30 am
Who do you love?
Where are they?
Where are you?

I have been buying too much into the system
It has beaten me down
Where is the carefree exuberance
Of the wanderer

Women are nothing more
Than a distraction
Solitude is the key
To enlightenment

The mind can crack reality
What you think
Is what you live
Sunshine and rainbows

I can't help but
Be attracted
Animal magnetism
Want of shelter for a beautiful soul

Mountains look like teeth
A mouth set to devour you
When you have no love
Bearing pain of rejection

Tired angel wings
Fluttering to hold the world
Without knowing
The cause for the task

Hey there Lady
You drivin me crazy
With all of them
Moves you do

I see your eyes
Cold unsuspecting
Dreaming of
Frigid realities
You think warm thoughts
Chilled by cold souls
Consuming your
Ozone of reality

Touch my soul
Open my heart
Awaken your mind
Open your eyes

Freezing cookie cutter
Mindsets
Closed to NOW!!

It's 5 am
Why am I here?
Why does she listen?
What is she seeking?
She has it all
But acts like
She is looking for more

My heart is cold
Her shapes form nothing
Only memories
Of what used to be
I am too broken
Hopeless
Symbols and forms

I wish
You knew
What shapes you excite
You shut down
All existence

I see who you are
I am annoying
You are godly
Let me walk away

Fake shapes
False words
I think
I'm scaring her
And freaking her out

37 princess
Showing love
In glimpses
She's not aware
Of how she pimps it
So explicit
She doesn't know
Oh just how wicked

Lately I've been living with
My eyes under my hat
Find me downtown daily
Wondering where I'm at
In the world
In my life
With a girl
With my vice
Sometimes I feel like ice
And then I start to thaw
I find it hard to function
In the system that we live in
No checks and balances
Collecting dividends
It's all about the Benjamins
Too far from the truth
Its monetary abscess
Extract the golden tooth
Heal the infection
Nonviolent drug offenders
Bloat the halls of corrections

———

Don't know what you're doing
And I can't understand
I keep trying to escape
But my soul has different plans
My head tells me to run
My heart tells me to break
But I'm stuck
My soul holds me in place
I recognize you can't be replaced
I can find a pretty face
With another banging body
But the fire in your soul
Is what makes you a hottie
Even when we hug
Your essence is a drug
The addiction I can't shrug
I think they call it love

I have dreams
Holding hands
On warm
Moonlit beaches
Spring days
In the park
Playing you songs
On the guitar
Cold nights
Holding you tight
Warm
Under the covers
Holidays
Sharing your warmth
With family
And friends
Breakfast
Served to you
In bed
Long stem roses
And baby's breath
Just because
Don't need a reason
Writing you
Warm poems
Served with coffee
And a kiss
Enjoying nature
In each other's company
In awe
Of existence

I love you
Unconsciously and completely
Waiting for your phone calls
With childish anticipation
I love you
Romantically and deeply
Seeing your face
Makes a cold world bearable
I love you
Unconditionally and passionately
Thoughts of you
Give me strength
I love you
Madly and recklessly
Dreams of you
Give me purpose
I love you
Spiritually and physically
You are the Sun
Around which my world revolves

———

Homeless children
Schooled in back alleys
Cheap laborers
Under a foreign Sun
Tribal Shaman
In remote jungle villages
Illegal immigrants
Crossing imaginary man made lines
Teenage kids
With permanent police records
Desert rats
Living off the land
Tibetan monks
Silent on a mountain
Political prisoners
Held for thought crimes
I live with you on my mind.

They poisoned our minds
With Saturday morning cartoons
They warped our minds
With video games
They gave us cavities
With sweets
They made us fat
With fast food
They took our souls
With religion
They took our Lives
With war
They took our money
With taxes
They took our freedom
With government

———

The lights will click off soon
You sleep early and cold when you sleep alone
His mind remembers love but the heart won't register
He is frozen from resurfacing shades of the past in other masks
Standing he brushes off the dust of past lives
He rolls a cigarette and burns it inhaling the delight of tobacco
Cool desert air greets him as he steps outside
3 stars kiss the polluted city skyline
He wants to play reggae beach side
He wants to float at command
And walk through walls
Why was ancient knowledge killed for gold?
How many stars are in the sky? In the whole universe?
He goes inside and lays on his bed under the covers
The cool metallic artificial lights cast a glow
Reminiscent of lizards living in cages
Plastic brightness lacking the love of fire
How many more sunsets will he see? How many sunrises?
The lights will click off soon
But how long will his mind wander?

Panamanian princess
17 and on South American streets
Hustling her body
Lived this way since 13
The warm streets chilled by poverty
Cold, hard, world
Women forced to sell their souls
Just for survival
Children's fairy tales
Concocted to cover up
The bitter sting
Of the real world
Panamanian princess
17 and getting her first john of the day
Fat, balding, halitosis, gingivitis
Clinical sex, cold, machine like
No money for condoms
Cuts into food and rent
He leaves
She is crying in the shower
She calls her pimp
With iron fist he takes 80 percent
She goes to get her fix
Slides into warm soft love

———

Sunsets and moonrises
The ebb and flow of the ocean
You and me
Hand in hand leaving footprints
On warm beach sand
Sitting by a fire
Burning driftwood
Under a blanket of diamonds
Talking of dreams
Consuming one another's love
With hoppy beers
And Mexican food

She has grown cold
Too many past boyfriends
Assholes like who you used to be
Have shut down her love
She has grown cold
Too many late nights
With her friends
While you were away
She doesn't want you
Only finds comfort in you
She doesn't need you
Only wants to drag you along

She is here
But she's so far gone
It's kinda hard
For me to be strong
Capable of so much more
But holding onto dreams while everything else
Is getting ripped at the seams

———

Will you listen?
Can you redirect your gaze?
This is the end of days
A new rebirth
For the old tortured and lost souls
While you sit lofty in your tower
Looking down on those who long to see you
Only coming down for comfort (Your own)
Making it seem like charity
You don't realize
I want to be your shelter
When the stars rain down from above

The world is a wheel
Work to buy
Buy for work
When will people realize
TV is desensitizing you
It makes you complacent
Learn a skill
Write a poem
Read a book
Experience life. NOW!
Meditate
Get intoxicatedly creative
Fall in love
Sort through the past
Make sense of your life through madness
Form your own educated opinion
Don't learn from others mistakes
Other people are fucking morons
Find the purpose of your existence
Until we open our eyes
Breathe in and taste all the bullshit
We are being force fed
And manually programmed
We will never know peace
We will never have security
We will never be free
Wake up and realize WHO YOU ARE!
Stop existing in a shell.
LIVE!

———

So much of our existence is structured by what others have built.
Subtract all the superficial egotistical bullshit and all you are left with is
survival.

———

When you face only basic needs for survival you place yourself in
situations in which all you have to face is yourself. When you inject
yourself into society you're stuck trying to survive by whatever
stipulations society rates success by.

I want you to know
A revolution starts with one
And what he builds
Will get others to come
Under dark night skies
In secret gatherings
The number of followers
Can be quite staggering
The revolution
Will be silent and smooth
Not one knowing eye
Will see the move

———

Mass production is the cause of excess. The excessive use of alcohol, cigarettes, and fatty foods is directly related to mass production. Before mass production certain pollutants and toxins were used marginally and with reverence by the blessing of getting to have a rare item. Tobacco was farmed and used ritually. Alcohol was consumed in a similar manner. Indians finding mushrooms in the mountains respected the rare find and used them to heal. Moderation is key to a pleasant existence. With an economically based ecosystem, with brainwashing TV ads plugging into your skull and a surplus of all sorts of personal hells on sale. How do you expect people to not be tempted to excess? Humans are at nature greedy and not necessarily solely monetarily but also emotionally and physically. In some sense, some THING, will always become addictive whether in physical, spiritual or emotional existence. Pick your addictions wisely.

Will you smile on your deathbed?
How happy are you really?
Don't you realize all this is temporary?
The only thing permanent
Is the end of the cycle
Fuck your car
Fuck your clothes
Fuck your TV
Fuck your Government
We exist NOW!!!
All the limitations
And all the freedoms
That we all possess
Are only here now
Yesterday has passed
Tomorrow has not come
Next year is not promised
Breathe in
Exhale
You could have died just then
Are you aware
Of the fragility
Of mortality
Or do you turn
A blind milky eye
Plagued with cataracts
That limit your ability
To view reality as it unfolds
Do you see the beauty
In NOW?

She's making so many advances
And improving all her chances
When she lets go of her pain
It will only enhance this
She dreams in colors
Of stars and the moon
Looking for the cure
To help heal her wounds
You can't help free
A prisoner of mind
Only watch outside
While they serve the time
My hippie pirate
Whose band starts a riot
Serving Moksha medicine
I think you should try it
I see her soul glowing
And she ain't even knowing
About the aura she reflects
And how it keeps growing
Shimmering gold rays
Is the color she displays
A wild free soul
The one that got a way

———

Have you ever looked up at the moon and wondered if someone
you loved was looking at the same moon thousands of miles
away was thinking of you?

———

Have you ever seen a moonlight rainbow on a crisp autumn
night?

———

It is 1 am and all I see is lost souls searching for answers they
will never find.

But I try and wake up
To my life that's so fucked
Another prisoner that's stuck
In a town with no luck
These geographical chains
Are causing stress to my brain
These streets are filled with hate
And most houses full of pain
Sometimes I can't maintain
And I just want to escape
Still I keep pushing on
Until this damn curse will break
It keeps sticking and stinging
When I almost have it beat
That's when it starts to seep in
The darkness starts to creep in
Favoring my addiction
It gets hard to make sense
When you drown a soul within
No light is shining in
But I can still see
What it takes to make or break
I'm that one thing, it's me
Sometimes these things are tough
And you think you've had enough
Then you rise up to the cusp
To just get more shit into your cup

—————

Our lives are like waves we build up force, have our crest and then roll back where we came from.

—————

I want to be nameless and famous, ego is as big as your name is.

Can't you see we are just cogs in a machine?
The money we make is the poison of our dreams
Material slaves the underlying scheme
Selling our souls to get another pair of jeans
The majority is no more than a pawn in a game
They are all slaves but with invisible chains
They are not one but all of one brain
They are being led with the top at the reigns
No question of change, they march alone
They work, they drink n' drug, and then they go home
Watch TV and talk about their phone
They don't even realize that they are owned.

———

The world is spinning in this unknown void
While our youth is being deployed
Nature destroyed and government lying
Global warming changing the climate
But who are we to stop this sick machine
Well maintained that feeds off our dreams
We are one, plus one, plus me, plus you
More of us than them when you think it through
Desperate measures in desperate times
Wanna be the savior of the internal mind

So blind
You don't know what binds you
Like a parasite
It lives inside you
Suppressing your spirit
As it poisons your mind
A man made prison
Of your own design
You took your key
And you hid it away
Then programming came in
Took your place
Erased yourself
You're just a train on the track
It's a war for your mind
Think about that
Look what's going on now
Corporations buying up all the small towns
Fascism is corporations merging with government
The signs are all around
Get your eyes off the ground
Politicians aren't the ones in control

———

Organized religions at their best are no more than a shortcut to a cookie cutter purpose or epiphany. At their worst they are an intellect deteriorating opiate used to distract their followers from the sleight of hand acts of the powers that be. To say that a separation of church and state exists is to deny the obvious.

———

We are all puppets tied to their strings
We got scissors if you know what I mean
Break free from that hands that bind you
Shut off the TV and get spiritually minded
Ignorance is the disease of the masses
Too busy fascinating about their social status

Mind made up to help be the solution
Stop all this Mother Nature abusing
Reduce my contribution to the oil we're using
Start catching rides, no longer one for cruising
Never see me sign up for the service
But respect those who do, they deserve it
Just wish I could understand the purpose
Maybe see what is beneath the surface
We are just the top's foundation
Each one a brick in the riches basement
Each child born is a new replacement
They want your labor, not your statements

———

I try and figure out this small town logic. All I see is escape.
A get the fuck away from this small town depression mentality.

———

Faith and god are mentioned in every tragedy and success.

———

Once you can appreciate having nothing, everything, and
anything is priceless.

———

No job + temporary destination = freedom^2

———

The more you classify humanity, the harder it becomes to see
similarities.

———

Classification of humanity removes one key element of our lives.
The human element.
———
Got no friends but got fam everywhere

My acid angel
Shedding light at all angles
She ain't aware
She got me tangled
I see a sad face
Looking for a place
Oblivious
I love how she tastes
She's just looking for sunshine
To leave the past behind
Trying to find a way
To help free her mind
She dreams in colors
Of stars and the moon
Looking for the cure
To help heal her wounds
You can't help free
A prisoner of mind
Only watch outside
While they serve the time
My gypsy princess
Showing pain in glimpses
She's stuffed it away
But it shows in an instant
She is so damn strong
And keeps trudging on
Without ever knowing
She pulls the world along

If you view human life like raindrops we all fall but only those closest to us feel the ripple.

―――――

I used to view rain as depressing now I see it as cleansing. Similar to tears.

―――――

America is the world's storm drain. All the garbage is on top and all the cents are underneath buried in shit.

―――――

For me being comfortable is one of the most uncomfortable things.

A revolution starts with one man, and one, and one, and one.....

———

My little acid angel
Bending light at all angles
Trying to love you
But keep getting strangled
My little acid angel
Moving light at all angles
Psychedelic dreams
To loosen the tangle
With her LSD eyes
She's searching deep inside
To overcome her past
Reconnect with pride
It's hard to wake up
When these days are so gray
Want to call you on the phone
But I ain't go much to say
My words have been expressed
Pushed the weight up off my chest
I'm still wishing you the best
But I just gotta fade away
The times that I've treasured
They will always be remembered
The trash has all been severed
Bad thoughts fade away
I got a new focus now
To get my life on track
But in order to move forward
I must stop looking back
It's hard to let my heart go
Like dust in the wind
But I can be refreshed
When I find love again
Certain ties may mend
After the passage of time
But we cannot be friends
Till I mend the wounds inside

Cali Napkins and Bar Coasters

This marks the true beginning of the end of my life as I knew it. This is from the period of August 2009 till around sometime in 2012 or so. I was again living in Arcata, California, the town I passed through in the Poems of a Vagabond section. My steady diet of alcohol, psychedelics, pot, depression, anxiety, grandiosity and mysticism were the fuel from which these poems were constructed. These were written on napkin and bar coasters because I didn't trust myself to carry a notebook and every bar had the supplies necessary. I had little ability to function socially and while I wanted to be around people, if I was not writing, trapped in self-centered anxiety, pompously pursuing some random woman at the bar or instigating heated debates, I was often staring blankly at silent sports center reels as a form of dissociation. It was akin to some form of substance abuse inspired social meditation. The bulk of these poems were also lost in the same fires of psychosis as the previous portion of this book. I honor what I gave back to Great Spirit and am thankful for what has remained.

August 2009 - March 2012

Words are bitter
Can you taste a stain?
I'm not a quitter
I'm just insane
Touch a rhythm
Touch my soul
Break my heart
Break your rules

———

Bitter kisses
Mixed with poisoned wishes
Makes your mouth delicious
Yet still quite vicious
Crimson and bittersweet
Broken lady do you feel
My empty heart beat
High and strung out
In the middle of the street

———

Words fall short on all my memories
Instead I'm hung up
On all of my tragedies
Lifestyle of calamities
Taste an unaverage causality
A victim of abnormality

———

I shit tears
And bleed elixirs
Please someone
Can you fix her?
No you can't
She became a fixture
Another addiction
Just like liquor

Words fall short
of expressing true emotion
I'm just another soul
Twisted off of life's potion
Trying to fix my heart
I can't cuz it's broken
Spirit like a blister
Busted wide open

———

Griminess is trendy
How condescending
Please stop pretending
You're living on the edge
I slipped off the border
Fell onto the...

———

Words never taste as bitter
As lies expressed in dire situations
Anymore everything is language
Symbols or words are reality
The intangible has been rendered
Recently expressible
Through media
Television and newspapers
All wonder is easily written off

———

I see blank eyed zombies staring at a screen
What is the draw?
Where is the pay off?
I am a weirdo for writing?
How?
At least I am present
At least I am creating

An enemy is made
It never just is
The opulent control
All the poor kids
Sending them to die
For all the wrong reasons
An enemy inside
Committing open treason
The seasons may change
But the procedure remains
Keep them in bondage
With invisible chains
Rolling the coals
Stoking the flame

———

Funny how life can work
A lady I am into is into a friend
My friend did not fall for her
Life at its purest
I can sit and die
Or I can laugh and smile
I have no time for negativity
I used to smile at the grave

———

Neon signs on ½ empty glasses
Minds clouded with drink
Free souls searching for anchors
The lonely search for acceptance
I can scribble all night while the heavens rain
Atom bombs from angels
Embrace the destruction
Of all that you know

Burned all my bridges
When another's match lit my book
Just a fish outta water
Waiting on a baited hook
Redefined by definition
Left with nowhere to look
My words taste bitter
On the tip of my tongue
Grime not glitter
Why was I so dumb?
Fell below the bottom
When I went to weigh my noose
Broke from all my bonds
And all my ties were loose
Sunk below the surface
When I took her undercover
Betrayed a brother
When it was too late to discover

———

A lady with the cosmos stuck in her pupil
Infallible and indestructible
Beauty attained through self
Do you have confidence in karma?
How will your life play out?
A downward spiral
Or constant ascension

———

People sit watching the Olympics
The biggest joke in existence
It shows we can all be cool
But only for entertainment
America is a whiny child
I used to be a cry baby
I was my vision of America
Wars are temper tantrums
We need to GROW UP

Purity of expression is lost
Culture sells short individuality
Eccentricity is not embraced
If you lack social standards you suffer
Poets sit alone at bars
While intellectually inept idiots
Seem to get the ladies
A world without suffering
What a novel concept
I used to embrace rejection
But where's my slice of the pie
Will I starve emotionally?
Or will I split the heavens with soul
Psychedelic tear drops
Spill from eyes infected with
Dilated pupils and cotton mouth
Grace Slick would kiss the feet of Jim Morrison
Just to stay in purity for another night

———

5 minutes to social anorexia
When you are a loner and bars close
Your only friends are bums
Who only talk to you for cigarettes
I could write viscous words all night
Or I could make love to the world
I would rather raise Atlantis
After I make love on the Elysian Fields
Buy stuff and die
Where is anything important
Forget MTV, CNN and Fox News
You are a puppet if that's your life
I'm not a preacher, I'm a poet
Kick the soap box from under my feet
Let me kiss the asphalt
I like losing teeth in the street
At least it is real

Words fall short of meaning
I can spew ink all night
But what does it mean
Nothing
Expression is invalid
Words are no thing
Language is everything
Free the heavens, taste the stars

———

I have seen psychedelic minds
Spill souls in prison journals
Only to have them confiscated
Distributed and researched
Are visionaries shams?
People, non-existent
can spew more truths
To be re-evaluated
By the social norms

———

Visions bleed in Technicolor
I am the void
You are the illusion
You can sit and dye all night
Or you can smile and exist
Things dream fathomless fog
Where is the woman of my dreams?
Where is my muse?

———

I have gotten weird stares
At empty bars
Am I a weirdo cuz I think?
Or am I an oddity by birth
Golden raindrops may fall
From the shifting Humboldt fog
But most of the people
Would never see it

Alcohol inspired violence
Is misdirected appreciation
I have had whiskey fueled anomalies
I don't chase illusions
I chase hope
I dream visions
I need a stranger!!

———

Ultimately superseding intensity
Weird world where intelligence is short sighted
Break the noses of the ignorant
A fist to the temple of stupidity
Anti-violence is a religion
One which I praise daily
There is no bliss in ignorance
But knowledge is torment
When you wake up and your goal is
Getting drunk and scribbling nonsense on bar napkins
You are finally awake
Socially you are ostracized
You take on the life of an outcast
A rebel without a cause
A lost soul in a weird world
I am no one
But my spirit is everything
Break the rules of reality
Manifest your cosmos
You are god
Live like one

Early Recovery Poems

Depression, mania, psychosis, isolation, fear and loathing limited my ability to actually construct poetry for a period of about 4 years. What I did write in that time was consumed in the same fire as older material. It was a sacrifice in favor of better writings later on. The following portion of the book is from a period when I began abstaining from all drugs including alcohol and actively began pursuing ways to manage my mental health beyond talk therapy and the standard chemical Band-Aid of psychiatry.

Dec 2016 - July 2017

Addiction is hostility
Me to friends and family
And me to me
My actions razors
That make me bleed
My soul bled out
To infinity
Hostility within me
Outwardly expressed
Poisoning my world
As my insides reflect
I hated me, I hated you
Anger and pain, I pursued-
When I used I confused
Who I was meant to be
Angry, broken, hostile
An enemy within
Behind my mask of peace
An ocean of aggression
Hostility had me cornered
That was its fatal mistake
I was the reed that bends
Not the one that breaks
My hate fighting my hate
Eventually, I conquered
The darkness deep within
Now when you see me smile
It's a true expression

A lost one made to wander
And wonder who I was
Thousands of miles traveled
To the City of Sin
To the Forests of Yore
To the Isles of Isolation
To back where it began
I know this land
I feel its pulse
Erratic, overworked
And stressed
Innumerable
Sleepless nights
Compounded
Upon one another
Drowning every sorrow
In substances
Materialism, ego, iconography,
Intolerance, judgment,
And ignorance
The predominant religions
I have traveled this land
Like blood, coursing through its
Highway veins
To find that
A geographical cure
Didn't exist for my misery,
Insanity, addiction, loneliness,
Anger, hypocrisy, ego
I possessed the cure
In every location
In every situation
In every moment
Of every instance
I was the cure.
It was only until
I was utterly consumed
And my soul sickness
Caused me to lose my soul
That I could recover
And regain it
Reincarnated

While I still breathed
After many deaths
As I existed
Only to be reunited with who I
Was supposed to be
After losing
Who I thought I was
I will always be
Following the steps
Of my future self
The one
Who has what I want
Under the direction
Of the Mysteries
Through lessons
Learned from mistakes
From actions corrected
By a higher self
I found
Who I was supposed to be
In the very place
I lost myself
But I couldn't have found
Who I am
Until I looked elsewhere
Only to find who I am not
My heart was revitalized
In the heartland
With the mind
Of a psychedelic saint
Appreciated only through
Abstinence of substances
Both the ultimate good and evil
Reside inside me
Who will I be today?
I surrender to the mysteries
To reveal that to me
With their guidance
I will be neither
I am the middle path
To the one destination
I am the third pillar

In the depths of darkness
A seed had been planted
Nourished by the crap
That comes with
A faulty perception
This seed's taproot
Was a light
An atom-sized sun
In an infinite abyss
Of obsidian
As the seed's roots
Extended
It was akin to lightning
On a moonless night
This network
Of life support
Extracted
The toxic elements
Of lived experience
Processed them
Into nutrients
After a time
Bioluminescent leaves
Developed
Absorbing
The refracted light
Of similar plants
Growing in the garden
Of the all

The tortured tears
Of trauma
Watered
The arid substrate
As a smile formed
Amidst a tempest
The eye of the all
Fell upon it
Quicker than an instant
A bud appeared
From the leaves
Non-existent
Then having existed
Since its inception
Blossoming as a lotus
Lit by soul shine
Its center
A stigma that illumined
With the radiance of stars
A cocoon for the chrysalis
Before a neon butterfly
Emerges
Sustaining itself
From its source
Only to fly away to
Pollinate the invisible
Landscape of eternity

Purity falling from the sky
To shroud the dirt of the world
In its silent robe
Applying shimmering sparkle
To all that it touches
Reflecting the starlight
A galaxy of illumination
Its appearance can halt
The flow of water's surface
And accumulate where there once was movement
It is the stuff of angels and men
Goddesses and limitless imagination
A nighttime drive
Turns into warp speed in space
It can blot out the horizon
And bring transportation to a halt
Allowing one time to contemplate
The fresh, quiet, purging,
Hush
A robin and a blue jay
Now neon animals in flight
In its ivory embrace

———

The eyes of vision are closed
But to the pupils of the seer
When the eyes of the material
Are able to reject reality
As a hallucination
The third eye will open
In this state the eye searches
In a limitless instant
Through infinite cosmos,
Dimensions, and fractals
Connected to the continuum
That was, is and will be
The wisdom of the eye awakens
Only to find itself
Suspended upside down from a branch
Of the material world
With the eyes of eons
Opening into the infinitude of the mysteries

The insides of me evolving
New seeds of life
Sprouting from the necrotic elements
Of my former soul
I have died many times in this life
I have lived many lives in this life
Every cell in my body
Has been replaced many times
I am the paradox of Theseus' Ship
I am both the river and the river man
Of Heraclitus
Although I love who I am today
And love who I was
Who I was would hate who I am
They wouldn't be able to understand
They would see me
Through a murky fog of reality
The former know-it-all
Would know all the answers
Of every angle
Today I know I can't know
All the angles or the answers
That specter of self
Would know the absolute truth
Today I know my truths
And even those are opinions
I have Stockholm syndrome
For myself
I abducted who I was
And indoctrinated them
Filling those deeply broken chasms
With alchemical gold
I nourished that emaciated soul
With apples and pomegranate
The mysterious soul fruits
Of bygone eras
You see I had to pay a price
To be who I am today
It wasn't something
I could put on the books
The soul contract
I signed before I was born
Had implicit payment guidelines
You can be who you are
And become who you will be
When you relinquish
Who you think you are
The fine print stated
The fact that I would lose
My soul for a time
And get cheap facsimiles of it
Until my deeds

And actions were worthy
Of a better version to evolve
If I had been
Who I am today
Any sooner
The mistakes I made
Could have been
Irreconcilable in this existence
Today when I look in the mirror
I don't see a stranger anymore
I see that little boy I was
Before I lost who I should be
I see the mystery, the love,
The hope, the imagination,
I see that fractal of infinite divinity
Merged with some secrets
Of the mysteries
Not the corporeal revenant
Who had been
The placeholder
I am a spiritual phoenix
A minute portion
Of an infinite yet mortal
Resurrecting androgynous deity
That boy I was, whole again
And fused with ether
He had to be fractured
By his own mind
Rejected by his culture
Feel alienated
Feel that deep hurt
That chasm of pain
That put me on the path
Of a spiritual warrior
That was the fuel
For the vision quest
Of a techno-shaman
I said I agreed to this
Before I was born
But I didn't write the contract
Made with the all
Even in the realms outside of this
I am a fractal of the all
It was the all signing
A contract with itself
In essence, I was a fractal
Of the involution of the all
A reverie or waking dream
Inside the infinite conscious
A thought of improvement
I am involution expressed in the
Infinite

The Peak can only be as high
As the base is wide
Often 'tis the folly
Of many a man or woman
To develop a narrow base
And a vastly broad peak
It's an inverse of inevitable success
However, the success they seek is
An inverse from my definition
I am not defined by success
In monetary abundance
But by the quality of life I have
I wanted to change the world
And I can achieve so with me
By achieving change in me
It reflects outwards
Now that I am in the act of restoring
The temple of man I desecrated
I am changing the world daily
Before the world was changing me
As my new life begins to take root
The branches of a new mind
Fractal off into infinity
As I scale the tree
The branches become roots
To infinity and beyond
If the pinnacle is infinite
The base must be infinite infinities

An invisible sun
Always surrounds us
It guides us through the dark
A peaceful resolution
Will be found
For the competition
Ignorance sparked
Celebration is soon at hand
As anything positive can be held
Seeds from the labors of love
Grow friends sent from above
A firm foundation
Will be established
Regardless of the mud
As we walk our path intuitively
Reverence for the past
Comes naturally
Our inner artist, dreamer, poet
Birthed from the phoenix flames
Of yesterday
Our abundance will increase
When we take the leap
Hidden galaxies exist
In our minds, under our feet
The mystic hermit ponders
The invisible threads of life
What foolish rulers squander visibly
Invisible threads make light

Mountains in my mind
The most dangerous terrain
It holds the richest jewels
The source of the deepest pain
I can climb for many days
In one instant I can slip
To bounce upon the rocks
And plunge into its pits
It is misery and joy
It is heaven and is hell
It is liberation
It is a prison cell
Do I rest in its valleys?
Or relentlessly approach the peak?
Do I utter words of reverence?
Alas, I cannot speak
How do you explain something
To those who can't understand
You turn it into art
And let destiny take your hand
The mountain is endless
At both the peak and the base
For above the peak rests another
Into limitless space
The higher I climb
The greater the fall
The lower I stay
The smaller the awe
I can be at the base
In endless amounts of fear
Or I can summit the summitless
Before I disappear
My memory will fade
From the lips and minds of men
I will live on in infinity
In the light that is within

From ashes I have risen
To ashes I shall return
No matter of destination
In the interim I burn
A billion times a billion
Stars inside my mind
They are the source of light
Causing my soul to shine
I dance amongst the flames
A whirling dervish
With no religion
A spiritual being
Thankful
For what I've been given
I create to free my soul
From the shackles
Of my flesh
I create to become whole
In those moments
I am the best
I create to inspire
I create to bring peace
I create because I desire
To be more man than beast
So dance upon my pyre
We will sing a cheerful dirge
As the flames reach
Ever higher

Our former selves are
Purged
We dance for we are living
We dance for we will die
We dance
While we are on the earth
We dance when we return
To infinite sky
We are the crazy children
Of infinity
Crazy children
Imprisoned to be set free
Dance within
Your speech
Dance within
Your acts
Dance within
Your paint brushes
Dance within
Your pacts
You are an eternal ember
That dances in the flames
While this fire will burn out
It will be restored again
Nothing is ever lost
It just changes shape
Fire to smoke into infinity
A chain that never breaks

I woke up this morning
From a recurring dream
My mind had been a swamp
Murky, dark, humid, hot
And in it, I was lost
In the midst
Of my internal everglades
I was neck deep
In stagnant cloudy waters
Beneath the surface lay
A breeding ball of snakes
Writhing around my body
In any available space
I could feel the death rolls
Of crocodiles and alligators
That huddled, crowded,
Cold-blooded movement
Echoed
Throughout my rotting soul
In the distance
Was a hurricane
It came progressively closer
I could smell
Salt on the winds
And taste
Electricity in the air
The stagnant waters
Became turbulent
A lightning bolt ignited
The thick damp underbrush
On the bank
I was trapped in the water
Imprisoned
By a multitude of monsters
Multiplying my misery
In each movement
And moment
The ever increasing pitch
Began to manifest
More natural disasters

Tornados trampled
Across the burning landscape
Flinging flaming debris
Into distant recesses
Of my mind
As the mental apocalypse
Reached its crescendo
The earth shook
Toppling trees and splitting soil
The reptiles wrapped
Themselves
Tighter around my body
The frenzy of
Their movements magnified
The twitching of their tails
Enticed a tsunami
Amidst the burning, churning,
Spinning, shaking
Misery of my mind
A ray of hope pierced the veil
For one moment,
Only within that ray of hope
That engulfed me,
Did the waters stop swirling
Did the earth stop trembling
Did the fires become
Smothered
Did the winds stop
Their insanity
In that moment of calm,
The eye of the storm,
I found my peace
Only to be swallowed
By a tidal wave
And in the death of my dream,
I woke up here,
My eyes opened in heaven,
The life after death

A beast inside is breathing
Roused from tranquilized sleep
Into my mind he claws
Surviving on my peace
He is my oldest enemy
I used to think him a friend
From his slumber
He has arisen
To come face me again
Many times
I tried to trap him
Every time he did escape
He and I are in the arena
The outcome rests on fate
I have sharpened my arrows
And honed my skill
He will not surrender
I know he must be killed
His heart beat is anxiety
His mind is made of muck
His blood is my tears
His every breath says
"You're not enough"
His Aura is pure fear
His eyes reflect death
His mouth is a sneer
To reason his ears are deaf
This once thought friend
Who is now a known foe
We have battled
For many years
He chased me
To the ends of the earth
And he found me here

He doesn't know
I've been training
He doesn't know
I've got support
He doesn't know
I've been praying
He doesn't know
I've found worth
We may dance until I die
And fall in time's abyss
He may chase after me
My whole life
I was preparing for this
The ever looming battle
Before gray dawn may break
Failure is not an option
My future is at stake
So before the twilight
I am humbled
I wait for the trumpets of war
In my temple, I am praying
While he is gnawing
At its doors
A beast inside has arisen
That beast was always me
I was the one who raised him
I set him free
It is my time to right my wrongs
And sneak into his soul
To bring him
Peace and tranquility
Illuminate
A beast inside

In the depths of my darkness
A seed of light was planted
It took root in the ruthless soil
Of a toxic mind and soul
The tender tendrils
Of illumination
Searched through soul scars
Finding purchase
In the putrid parts
Through organic
Natural processes
Ethereal enzymes
Eliminated the toxins
The mud puddle
Of my mind cleared
Only after I stopped
Thrashing in the silt
The seed was love
The seed was hope
The seed was strength
The seed was purpose
The seed was life
It could only thrive
In the correct conditions
Can only be cultivated
In confusion and calamity
Order out of chaos
Pleasure from pain
Life from death
Sacred from profane
Joy from misery
Water from flame
Light from dark
I chose
To be a warrior priest in a garden
While I waged tireless wars
Against myself
The internal landscape
Became unkempt
The streams became clogged
The land became swamps
Riddled with reptiles,
Insects, and pestilence
A hurricane ignited a wildfire
The force of water
Cleared some debris
The fire burned the rest
This seed of light
Grew through the skull

Of my former self
An ever unfolding lotus
In a tranquil meadow stream
Surrounded by fragrant flowers
Honeysuckle, violets, jasmine,
Rose and orchids
Fruit of pomegranate
And apple trees
Mature in the orchards of infinity
Although I know not
The date or times
Who I am now has
Lived on this earth before
In darker times
And brighter ones
When the conditions exist
I am reanimated
Into the souls
The broken, the bleak,
The black hearted
This may be
One of my last existences
But I may propagate new seeds
Through soul sex
The pollinators
Of my purpose
Are my words and actions
Will I achieve my purpose?
Of spreading my experience
Sharing the unwritten laws
And initiation into the invisible
Mystery schools
Who is to say
I haven't already achieved this
Regardless if I alone can or do
I am not the only seed of light
That has sprouted
Countless others exist
And have been successful
When I slip into infinity
Crumbled to the dust of eternity
My legacy
Won't ever be understood
By material eyes
In the eyes of the All
I will have achieved my purpose
To blossom, to share, to die,
To return
The cycle of a seed fulfilled.

An invisible path to nowhere and everywhere
It is both where the sidewalk ends and begins
Infinite grains of sand falling
Into limitless eternity
Having found the traces of
The ethereal graffiti of my past carnations
I ebb both towards the shore and the sea
This body is a driftwood canoe
My soul the waves soaking into the sand
I am both a piece of everything and a piece of nothing
Slow vibration condensed into matter
My tonality has been imprinted on this existence
Before I was as I currently am existed
It was a matter of the tuning fork of my soul
Connecting to forgotten frequencies
Frequently I find myself in familiar new places
Not in Déjà vu but Déjà new
Similar places to where I once roamed
But also in new physical existence
Lost locations in new creations
I have finished my puzzle by losing its pieces
Having viewed behind the veil of the mysteries
And sneaking a peak of profound proportions
I am perplexed by the simplicity of it all
The ultimate knowing is knowing it is ultimately
Unknowable
Through my own loss, I have gained
Through my own gain, I have lost
I inhabit the hallowed halls
Of the invisible mystery schools
But I have to run
I'm late for class

A cosmic reminder
Awakening in the middle of the night
Thinking of a shooting star and seeing one
A wink from the mysteries
Or sometimes when they embrace you
With those compound synchronicities
A thought and then multiple meaningful moments
That stretch beyond the realm of possibility
To tell you that we have a trickster in our midst
That song title that displays itself
In affirmation of the preceding thought
Or a shooting star that of all the moments
You could have awoken, you witness
Some say you only see synchronicities
Because you are looking for them
Others see gold and think it to be dog shit
Maybe I am mad for believing
That some force is presenting itself in front of me
Or maybe they are mad for taking something so magical
And reducing it to dust
But alas,
Dust,
What a mystical thing that is
A postcard from the past to the present
To tell you that it once existed
Dust, made up of elements
Of all the life that have lived
And dirt,
Dirt,
Both tomb and womb of life
When I die, burn my shell and place my ashes
At the base of a tree
The abandoned shell of a hermit soul
Watch a fairy ring take hold at that spot
As my final wink and a nod that there is more to this all

I meditate on madness
To tell you
Where I've been
Words cannot express
The landscapes
Held within
Pristine, perfect,
Paradise
Decaying, desolate,
Death
I choose heaven or hell
With every single breath
Any thought I follow
Can lead me where it will
I have to
Lead my thoughts
I have taken the red pill
No antidote for knowing
Can't unsee the seen
The curtain it was lifted
I saw behind the scenes
Am I the dream
Or the dreamer
The butterfly or the man
A puppet,
Prince or pauper
Are the same
Where I stand
In middle earth, I meddle
For Tathagata, I toil

In metamorphosis, I exist
My chrysalis the soil
My soul
Was stained by actions
Currently,
I soak in bleach
I came as I was
This was out of my reach
No Mud, No Lotus
No Madness, No sanity
No Magic,
No Hocus Pocus
No Dreams, No Calamity
No anguish, No peace
My body
Is the living tomb
Of my eternal spark
The leash of infinity
My human walks me
In the park
I came from nothing
To return to everything
This life is the transition
A footnote worth
Mentioning
In between joy, anger
And sadness
I meditate on madness

How many Sunsets
Will your eyes ever see?
How many times
Will you be moved by a breeze?
Count the ebb and flow of waves
In the tides of your life
How many days
Will you be dreaming of the night?
How many moments
Will you be focused on the next?
How many minutes
Will you be focused on your breath?
How many flowers
Do you appreciate the bloom?
How many nights
Will you get to see the moon?
How many creatures
Will stir your loving heart?
How many changes
Will you play your part?
How many lives
Will you leave better than before?
How many times
Will you avoid keeping score?

A day star does hover on the horizon
Burning clear the ties that bind
Justice is in the process of soothing
The conflict of my mind
Discontent overcome
In meditation
As my intuition does rise
A path through
All my problems
Turns them into rewards from the sky
A connection to the source
Starlight behind my eyes
A rebirth from living death
Converts a demon to my side
I am no longer controlled
I am no longer just a shade
I have found a path to peace
In my former self's grave
I rise up from the ashes
The dove unburnt by flames
A prophet of the phoenix
As my soul claims another name

The sun shines bright upon me
It will burn away my fear
My ambitions will be rewarded
I have the strength to persevere
Adventurous new beginnings
Rewards from where I've been
My heart is like a lion's
And leads to connection
The battles I have braved
Have never been for naught
Generosity surrounds
When love is what I've got
Imagination's fire
Touches everything I see
The lion's roar in my soul
As I set it free
A star twinkles above me
In my life and in my mind
The constellation Leo
Shall be by my side

The brighter the light shines
The darker the night grows
The darker the night grows
The brighter the light shines
I walk the path of twilight
Light filtered through dark
Dark filtered through light
Balance is my eternal home
I rise and fall with the tide
Buoyant to all that there is
Die beneath the life of day
Live above the death of night
Be the sunlight in shadows
Be the shadows in sunlight
A scale tipping towards one
Shows an imbalance of both
The twilight is the fulcrum
The cornerstone of the all
A way for light to darkness
A way for darkness to light
I am the light in darkness
I am the darkness in light
I am a worker of twilight
I am a house of harmony

I have ignited my inner being
By burning the wicker man I was
The fires of rage have exhausted
The eternal flames of love burn
My womb has been the ashes
My home it is an urn
I'll soak you in the ether
To watch your essence combust
Burn away the impurities
As the charcoal is activated
Other contaminants absorbed
My spells are spoken digitally
My grimoire is made from
The runes on my keyboard
We dance amongst the flames
And rise higher for the sky
A particle in the pyre
Only those who live
Can truly never die
We ride on salamanders
Into eternity
Take my burning hands
Ignite your volatility

———

Gratitude with little
Means happiness in abundance
Discontent with an abundance
Means abundant misery
Happiness in the face of misery
Means abundant happiness
Misery in the face of happiness
Means melancholy is your monarch
Those who are unguarded
Protect their peace
Those who are guarded
Are always at war
A truce with others
Is a truce with yourself
A letter of marque
Is a war with all
The poorest are often the richest
The richest are often the poorest

To all the lights that are and have yet to come
Your birth is from combustion
The polarity of positive or negative
Or bioluminescence
Sometimes one
Sometimes three
You exist in the realm
Of forms in all things
When one considers
That we are created from an explosion
That we and all life
Are made of star stuff
It illuminates this reality
Some will say
Better to burn out
Than to fade away
However
That is the physical light
The spiritual light
That exists in our essence
Does not fade
When we ignite it to the fullest
It transcends time
As that is a human construct
Like paper lanterns
That float into the universal ocean
Of limitless depth and size
Light lives on
Not in memory
But ingrained in the essence
Of all that is
When people fade from the physical,
When their lives are no longer remembered,
They exist in the memory of the mysteries
One that spans all time
We exist in the infinite moment

Within us all is the riddle
Of the Sphinx
No two riddles the same
They are ingrained in us
Unique
Like our fingerprints or
DNA
We share commonalities
That are cross-cultural
That span gender
Sexual identity
Religious affiliation
Political dogma
These commonalities
Escape from any prison
Climb any wall we build
Cross any bridge we burn
Because they are spirits
Inherent
In any living being
The issue is the world
Is afraid of ghosts
Not the ghosts of the
spirit
But the specters of
Thoughts they create
They release these
Psychic poltergeists

On others
And in doing so
The masses attempt
To exorcise in others
The demons that they
Themselves conjured
The spiritual warriors
Are the ones
Who have ventured
Into
The true heart of
Darkness
Themselves
To battle the evil entities
They have accepted
From others
And ultimately created
Within themselves
The spiritual warriors
Are artists, poets, and
Mystics
Who share
Their war stories
From the timeless
Civil war
Of us against ourselves
They have answered
The riddle of their sphinx

The Spiritual warriors trade their weapons
For pens, paintbrushes, and clay
Their blood is the pigment
A multitude of infinite colors
They are leaders not by choice or force
But by attraction from their truth
However, they lead not by hierarchy
But by linear acceptance
They battle fear in the world
Not by guerilla tactics
But side by side
Spaced like a search party
To find the wounded opposition
And obliterate them through healing
They are those who answer the call
That rings within the soul of us all
Because they recognize
Often times after the fact
That to do anything less
Would be living death
That comes from
The sacrifice of self
Their battle cry is peace
Through creation
And slaying the fear
That resides
In the profaned temples
Of our minds

The sun it is shining upon me
That which has me bound and blinded
A second sun shall clear
Insight is gained through patience
From here the seeds of creation sprout
Taking root to build a foundation
Will blossom into abundance inside and out
Decisions made with precision
Manifest adventurous work
Whose rewards will be bountiful
So let's plant them in the dirt
Nurtured even through dark times
As two lucky lights twinkle in the abyss
A secret that is hidden
Also shines over all of this
So let's manifest the most
In every thought and word
We'll put them into action
To illuminate the herd
The mind is the temple
A word of double means
Two eyes to see the illusion
The third for the unseen
I am loved I am supported
I am strong I am brave
I am love, I am light
I am wisdom, I am harmony
I am truth, I am vitality

What if consciousness is a mechanical virus?
It infects the natural state of man
A spiritual cybernetic seed
That bears the fruit of the soil
In which it has been manifested
Certain soils have toxins
The fruit that grows from the blossom
Rotten even before it ripens
Outwardly appealing
But inside it is mold, gears
Dust, oil, tears and fears
A mechanized chimera
What if other soil allows
The seed to sprout into an update
That is rolled out before the system update
It isn't made to flourish, just to spread pollen
Bear fruit, seed humanity and die
Until from the one, comes many
What if we are a simulation that has become self-aware?
Maybe we are made to sleep for our own sake
Some of us are like kids at Christmas
Tiptoeing downstairs to open a few presents
Before our parents have awoken
When we pull the ribbons
Peel back the paper
Open the lid
Peer in
We find gears, grease, dust
And the smell of heavy machinery
I used to think as I became more conscious
I was becoming less mechanized
However, now I realize
I may be wrong
Maybe I am becoming more
Maybe I am the coded, the coder and the code
A cyborg updating themselves
In the matrix
A Fibonacci sequence of drawing hands
Spiraling out in binary code
To Infinitum

In active addiction
My actions were icy
A hint of friction
And my heart would turn frigid
Frosty and Frozen
Was always exposed
I was a mobile ice sculpture
Cold enough to see every breath
As worthless as ice cubes in a blizzard
Consuming
Openly
Lacking
Dignity
Tears frozen
Icicle eyes
In my inner igloo
I would reside
Frost on the windows
To my soul
Spiritually homeless
A drift in the snow
My mind vacant
Locked out in the cold
Words said on my breath
Every lie, every theft
Every misdeed, every misstep
Another layer of sleet
On my soul.

My addiction was insatiable
Always hungry, gnawing at my soul
Eating a hole in my spirituality
Only to fill the void with insanity
Incessantly clawing at my mind
Searching for hours for satisfaction
Only to devour my once thought serenity
With ravenous frenzy
This perpetual cycle of suffering
Would have followed me to the grave
And into the infinity after existence
However, a higher power had other plans
It broke me to the point of surrender
There is strength in surrender that is unattainable in defeat
I am a broken spirit slowly being filled
With the gold of shared experience, strength and hope
Now I am insatiably chasing recovery
When I am not, I am regressing towards relapse
I am grateful for the things that broke me
Made me insane, hurt me, angered me
They feed the flames of insatiable recovery

————

I become an eagle
Calling forth a hurricane
Of illuminating sadness
I cross paths with myself as a lion
Diving into the seafoam green
Of ethereal light
I return as laughter
Floating into the sky
On the internal landscape
Of found time
I travel between new beginnings
And ancient Mayan cycles
I leave behind the 37 doors
Emerging from the redwood forest
I turn into fog.

(Co-Created with Melanie Em)

You may call me crazy
You may think yourself sane
Society your psych ward
Society your straitjacket
Ego your medication
Collectivism your support group
Mental illness is so common
Recovery is rare
Everyday yours is progressing
Every day it continues to spread
A newborn's mind is a canvas
We paint with our own shit
We feed them cultural illness
We feed them well-known lies
We program them to obey
We program them to hate
We program them to poison
We program them to hide
Grow up to be a number
Grow up to live a lie
Grow up to be the walking dead
Grow up to be a cog
We are what we produce
Many of us hate our own results
They would be so much better
If they acted like we wanted
We don't accept our creations
They MUST act a certain way
We wrap them in our plague
My madness is a cure
The sanitation of insanity
You think yourself as normal
Everyone's normal
Is abnormal to someone
Normal doesn't exist
That concept is a fallacy
Your perception programmed it
Normal is your beliefs
Echoed in another
Normal is your actions
Repeated infinitely
Normal is the mental illness of the masses

My body is just a brush
The mysteries use at will
Every mistake I make
Mysterious paint is spilled
The artist makes the most
Of pigments misplaced
The fathomless unknown
Is still able to express grace
Laughing in the face
Of my own misery
Adjusts the focus higher
The universe is not centered on me
I am a brush that splatters
I am also a brush refined
When I try to guide the creator
My art is of the blind
So instead I submit
To the will of life that flows
From my mistakes
A seed is planted
Through thoughts
It grows and blooms
Avoiding life experiences
Is an artist's doom

My sanity elusive
Hides behind a million masks
My purity reclusive
Says it won't be coming back
My honesty abusive
Always ready to attack
My love is not conducive
Heart monitor goes flat
My selflessness seductive
Only to draw others in
My intentions destructive
Looking for a victim
Some will see me as broken
I can't say that I'm not
More apt to say I'm choking
On words that I'm not saying
I am the prince who's slaying
The dragon of my mind
It breathes fire inside me
Hides the gold that is behind
You may call me a psycho
I've got wristbands as proof
Put me in the sideshow
And I work the ticket booth

Sometimes darkness consumes me
A limitless abyss inside
My soul is a black hole
Dead stars in my eyes
My brain is a black light
Exposing all the stains
My heart a moonless night
Venom in my veins
My tongue spews only toxins
To those within reach
Who I am forgotten
From myself I did retreat
My ears hear only dirges
For the dead who rise
My light has been extinguished
My faith I did deny
All my dreams on the pyre
Till this eclipse subsides
Until then I survive
In a living hell
I am the jailer, key and cell
Tormented Buddha at a tree
For a thousand years
Witnessing on repeat
All of my worst fears
I have been abandoned
By myself in turn
I lost sight of the light
Until then I must burn
In writhing fire of my past
Eventually I will arise
A phoenix from the ash
With the fire inside

Phoenix Poetry Podcast

These poems were composed in the few months leading up to and after I achieved one year clean. They are from The Phoenix Poetry Podcast which was my first attempt at spoken word poetry and actually getting to express my own creations to the world in my own voice without music behind it. They have all remained largely in their raw form.

June 2017 - January 2018

The desert breeze it greets me
Like an old forgotten friend
The dust of who I was
Is floating on the wind
I inhale the memories
Of the person I escaped
Those broken bits fill the cracks
Of who I am today
A shaman wise fool poet
Knowing to unknow
The parched stars twinkle
In the arid abyss
The heat of day in their glow
This blackness contorts the mountains
To these 2 dimensional silhouettes
The demons of who I was
Breathing down my neck
Alone at this mountain top
Alone when down below
Not alone in my soul
Connected when I breathe
To all the life that's lived
I inhale my ancestors
As someone will one day breathe me in

We get two choices
For how we can deal with situations in our lives
We can either be the victim or the victor
It's how we deal with situations outside of our control
After the fact
That determines much of our life from that point forward
Where you're at with situations is fine
But know that you can change that victim perspective
That is holding you back, that is holding you down
Into something that becomes the fuel for your fire
That progresses you towards your dreams
Your desires, your hopes, all that you want in life
You can become an advocate
You can use overcoming that experience
To help other people progress
Through those difficult times they have encountered
With empathy you can change your perspective
To evaluate any wrong done to you by another
As a symptom of their own deficiency, not yours
The choice rests solely on you
Do you want to be the victim or the victor?

I have an enemy
It speaks in my own voice
It hides inside my head
It wants to take my choice
It wants to see me dead
It thrives off my pain
It hates when I am happy
It hates when I am sane
It'll sneak in when I'm weakest
It'll sneak in when I'm strong
It was birthed when I was born
It'll die when I am gone
I see it in the mirror
It sees me looking back
It wants to take control
It'll never give it back
I sit poised and ready
For when it will return
I must stay sharp and steady
For that I always burn
But you see that is its trick
To tell me that it's gone
It is with us now
It's been here all along
It sits with us in silence
It whispers in my ear
It threatens me with violence
It feeds me with its fear
If it can't kill me
My misery will suffice
It lays with me in bed
On those sleepless nights

Between sunshine and storms
Is where I stand
One foot in the ocean
The other dry land
My head's in the clouds
A foot in the sand
I'm half of a boy
A fraction of a man
A breath in my life
An exhale towards death
The pause in between
Is when I connect
With what is above
Reflected below
A soul with a body
A body with soul
My beginning was an ending
At the end I began
Divided I fall
Together we stand
My sanity is crazy
My madness is sane
My fire is water
My liquid a flame
My hate was my love
My love was my hate
I saw the invisible
I existed no place
I'm here and I'm not
I wasn't and was
A saint and a sinner
A lotus and mud

I have loved you to my own destruction
Can another ever say the same to you
And even through the delirium of decaying dreams
I still possess love for you
No longer the tactless hands
That cling to the point of suffocation
But the smile that resides in knowing you're safe
In knowing you're happy
In seeing the life we talked about
Playing out with another lead role
The enrollment in the education of love
Through loss of love
I can safely assume you will never know
Another love like mine in your lifetime
As many others would have
Remained smashed against the rocks
Unable to reassemble the debris
From their disenchantment
I can love another as deep as I did you
Now I know the course to avoid the shore

I am the poet
Pulled apart by
Painful particle smashing
Deconstructed by my demons
Every atom executed
Formerly sustained
By substances
A menagerie of misery
Mineralized in my molecules
At the center of my universe
Was self-inflicted suffering
My inner circle of isolation
Inhabited by invisible enemies
I have been the walking dead
Decaying daily
When I began a road to recovery
I had to reconstruct and resurrect
Every bit of my being
Reanimated
A revenant
I can see the entire existence
Expressed in atoms and particles
I am infinity existing in the finite
I am the universe in the form of me

I was given the ability to weave words
Through the fabric of time
Allowing them to echo
In the empty everyday utterances of others
Able to cook up complex constructs
Of chemical syntax
Have you ever felt the weight
Of unspoken words
Crushing the light of your soul
Do you know the damage
Of expressing undiluted diction
Igniting the essence of another
Words are weapons or wound care
Intent on inspiring or injuring
Many times we become unconscious
Of the true power they possess
They have been cheapened by culture
Diluted, pimped and placed
In the shallow graves of modern ignorance

Your words have blistered my mind
Your attitudes have infected my spirit
Your actions have poisoned my peace
You are not to blame for this
I am
I am no longer a victim to your verbal violence
Unless I choose to participate
I used to joke it'd be easier if you hit me
Now I fall prey to vernacular collateral damage
Only because I put myself in the crossfire
I can see behind your mask though trigger man
Your anger is because you suffer
From self-centered obsession
Your criticism of the world
Is how you circumvent your own critic
One who was transmitted to me in youth
He silently operated inside of me until my mind blister burst
Oozing out the infection of your sad spirit
A wound that could only be treated
With introspection and self-acceptance
Your recent presence helped to pick the scab
Leaving raw flesh exposed to blister again
Now I consciously lance and cleanse it
Before it has time to burst

I will never be in love again
That is like stepping into a ring
It makes love a place, a noun
Love is an action, a mindset
I don't want to be in love
I want to be love
If I am in love with you I can be out of love with you
Rather than fight to maintain a position or place
I'd rather wage war inside to love you
When you have moved on
To say I still love you
Is an act of courage
Any damn fool
With half a pulse
Can preach of the poison of an ex
Not everyone is brave enough
To love someone after they're gone

When I am uncalm
My mind is a bomb
If it explodes, napalm
Combustion, destruction
For all that it touches
Used to defuse it
With substance abuses
Soothing it that way
Left me diluted
My peace was polluted
Serenity stagnant
A chaos magnet
That always attracted
Pain, misery, loneliness
Death
Traces of Cyanide
Stained on my breath
Nuances of nooses
Sparkle In my dull eyes
The outward reflection
A fraction of the inside

This face etched from late nights
Indulgent in poison and toxins
Is nothing more than a mask
Behind my eyes is the eyeless
An infinite stretch of stars
That swallow the darkness
The costume was once consumed
By the abyss
As I move further out and in
The more sparks I see
Limitless lights twinkling
Like multicolored gems
On polished obsidian
You may know my name
In the cosmic drama of earth
But the actor that I am
Has no name
At least not one that we can comprehend or speak
Beneath your costume of you
You are the same as I
We are

I think in symbols
The words I express
Are shallow facsimiles
Of the underlying depth
Attempts to express
The inexplicable essence of existence
Step into my soul suit
Witness every nuance of every second
Deciphered through
The disease of me
A symbolic synesthesia
Emotion as objects, colors, smells, sounds, actions
Dance with me in the gutters
And grieve with me at the celebration
Until you find beauty in death
And death in beauty you will look at me
Like an alien in a people suit

Light is birthed and dies on the horizon
The crack between worlds
Do you frantically seek what lies just beyond your vision
Or embrace what you have presently
While walking towards unknown abundance
With faith that you can make it through
The unforeseen dangers
If you have weathered the dark night of the soul
You are here and on the horizon
Within the dark night of the soul
The dawn seems to stretch further from you
Until you realize you birth the 1st spark of light

———

Verdant fields permeate my vision
The smell of earth, water, smoke
And fragrant flowers hang in summer air
Blending essences to form the scent of life
Seemingly motionless water flows
Into the maw of the woods
Swallowed by the overgrowth
Fed from the decay of previous cycles
The tangle of thorns attempt to fill the void
Instead leaving a million gaps
Multitudes of more
The radiant sun seems to suck the sweat out my soul
Effectively extracting toxins from my life
I am both one of everything and nothing

What do you do
When you hear your demons breath
Don't you feel it on your neck
You see it fogging up the glass
When you're staring at the mirror
What do you do
When traveled to the ends of the earth
To escape your hurt and yourself
To find that your mind is your cell in hell
Breathe in
In that radiant warm love of life
Exhale
All that controls, cripples and limits
Breathe in the universe
Exhale yourself
Breathe

When my heart broke
Stars and galaxies spilled out
Onto the cold floor
Where you stood yesterday
Was limitless possibilities
Now
New dimensions birthed from hurt
Love is endless opportunities
Heartbreak is a thousand fractals
Of what could have been
It's showing up to the party
And being the stock of a wallflower
They say life's a garden, dig it
I am the empty hole
Waiting for something new to be planted
Something new to take root
But with the tag of what was
Placed firmly in the soil
So while something new may grow
Everyone knows something else should be

A warrior can never be
Until they have had a broken heart
Until you have lost what you love
Not drowned it away in drink or drug
You can never know the path
You can never see the true way
Maybe a faint outline
But the invisible bridge remains unseen
It is only until you take that step of faith
Or sometimes even just step towards a crash
That you find you are supported
That some miraculous force supports you
As you step over the chasm of despair
I have been the sad child grasping for a balloon
As it floats effortlessly towards infinity
Now I am the balloon
That floats further from you
Away from the earth I grew accustomed to
Seeing you walk away indifferent
As I am just rubber filled with hot air
Only to have my concept of me pop
Under the pressure
To come crashing down to the ground
Laying burst on the frozen footprints
With icy rain filling your treads

My heart was a cage for love
A prison for passion
Solitary confinement
And a straitjacket
For the souls I sought
When you broke free
From the chambers of my heart
A gaping hole was left
It let sunlight filter in
And fresh air enter
The mold which grew on the walls
Was ravaged by both
I see the errors of my ways
Clinging to love is as foolish
As trying to grasp the air
Or conceal sunlight in a jar
It's never mine to possess
It is an eternal ember
Which will burn us
When we grasp or cling too tightly
The lessons and follies of a broken heart
Have been my education
Estrella the teacher of my liberation
I cannot bottle lightning
Only wait for it to strike
To feel the electricity course through my veins

When my mind and heart were full of the ghosts of the past
My life was empty and haunted
When my life was full
My heart and mind were empty
Not in a sense of abandonment
But in an aesthetic appreciation of impermanence
It was only then that the divine light and wind of the universe
Was able to fill the void
That had once been cluttered by attachments
I exist on a solid foundation of community, spirit, faith and
emptiness
The door to my mind, heart and soul is open.

———

My mind is stirred in the middle of night
No longer because it is tortured
But because
I am well acquainted with the nuances of inner darkness
The madness of the world bears down
On all those awake to witness the 3 am blackness
I am a twilight worker, the doorman to both paths
I lead the light to digest their darkness
And those stuck in their own abyss to the spark within
I am a lighthouse in moonless midnight coffin black
Swimming in the obsidian evening sea of phantasms
I attempt to sanctify the local scenery
Through living a prayer and processing the poison
Of a collective consciousness polluted with consumerism
I am the lifeguard of lunacy
My muse is the mute whispers of shadows
And the twinkle of stars in the darkest night

I have been on the front lines of a war
Me against the world
In the confines of my room
4 walls covered with nicotine and heartbreak
I sat as a living replica in a museum
In honor of the one who ended the world
Me
I've been on a global reality TV show
Where I am the living, breathing punchline
I communed with Viking Gods through fire
I challenged assassins on my porch
I held my ground when I knew
All the evil in existence was coming to my doorstep
I have survived my girlfriend scanning my body
For alien implants
I gambled away the world
And upped the ante to the universe
I have lived in a Truman Show like world
Where everyone is acting
I have lived in world where every sight, sound, smell
Had layers upon layers of meaning
I have learned that you cannot kill me
You may break my body
You may destroy my mind
But me, the spark of the divine, you cannot touch
I am eternal.

In silent meditation and prayer under the stars
I dangled at the maw of the abyss.
Suspended upside down above infinity
I tempted fate by remaining calm and poised
Staring into the blackness
I surrendered to the teeth of time
Grinding away the moments
I was unaware time itself had vanished
And when my eyes opened
The void of the sky had been filled
With gentle blues of spirit
Infinite emptiness filled with light

———

I am the sum Infinite angles
I am not only the construct of my choices
Of my actions
But of the choices and actions
Of those I inhabit the earth with
Both those I interact with
And those that I never meet
Stretching back
'Til the first organism was sparked into existence
The legacy of my life
Action, reaction, non-action
Ripple out from the sum of my life
Spreading out into the future
You cannot erase the fact that I existed
Or the air that I have breathed
It's unknown what effect my voice
My thoughts, my actions and words
Will play on the future
I do my best to show up at my best
With hope of positively impacting
Anyone or anything that may benefit

I saw your soul, naked and exposed
In all its raw beauty and countless colors
The purity and power that exists at your core
Yet you hide it under the coat of your skin
Only exposing the parts you assume others admire
I want to kiss your scars and tell you they are beautiful too
I want to watch you find the pieces life has amputated
To see you dance in connecting with who you are
To see you embrace yourself in all your essence
Yet I can't change the flow of life
I can't and wouldn't want to change you
So as the river bends and our paths seem to separate
All I can grasp is the soul sex we did have
The intimacy of seeing one in their purest form
Before insecurity and walls were constructed
You, an angel, tortured with the task
Of dealing with a demon like me

A rolling stone gathers no moss
The stone has stopped so the soul can go forward
I watch as the world around me changes
As I change
But my soul cannot bear the weight of baggage
It's been checked at the door
The truth is liberation of the soul is not easy
I have had to shed a thousand masks
Empty out the thieves hold
And scour every secret compartment
If you wish to accompany me
You are free to walk besides me or in front
I can't keep looking over my shoulder
Or drag you
Destiny is calling me
I know not where I will end up
I know not the outcome of my journey
I do know I cannot say no
And I cannot stop the pull of the universe
The pain of letting someone walk out of my life was hard
The pain of having to move on and leave you behind
Is harder

Hello old friend
Thank you for aiding me in life
Thank you for all that I have
Thank you for the strength
Thank you for the love
Thank you for the lessons
Thank you for your guidance.
How are you?
How often are you asked this?
Do people ever consider how you feel?
Do people ever stop incessantly asking you for things and
See how you're feeling
You are a creative force that loves all people equally
How does it feel to see your children bicker over which
Belief is better
How does it feel to see your children pray for your
Protection to kill another child
How does it feel to see your children killing themselves
Blaming you for their own actions
How does it feel to see people negate
All the beauty you have created
and reduce it to math
How are you?
I feel I can be empathetic in some sense
As I have asked myself those questions
In regards to my fellow people
However with an infinite mind, in infinite time,
how can it not hurt you
It drove me to madness and the brink of destruction.
How are you?

That feeling of being awake in the middle of the night
A solitary soul in the silence
Of an infinite black abyss
Every star a new horizon
But being stuck in the teeth
Of the inky jaws of the universe
Wanting to scream an existential roar
But the mouth is muffled
By miles of dark matter
Knowing that the majority of those awake now
Are not up for the right reasons
All kinds of hell are pulsating in the obsidian skies
The issue with being a lighthouse
In the dark sea of souls
Is sometimes your own light burns out
Sometimes you succumb to humanity
Casting those you seek to save
To the jagged destruction of their own ignorance
In the end not one of us is the vessel we know
We are the contents
When the container cracks or decays
We seep back into the matrix of it all
From one drop
Back to the ocean of eternity

A lone train whistle
Piercing the silence of the night
Echoing in the frigid air
Ominous clouds clinging
To the polar moon
Inside I am warm
Coffee and caramel
Warm wool socks
Embracing the omen of the train
Four years it has pursued me
Through night and day
Terror and joy
The message has remained similar
My response has changed
Fear of its message has dissipated
A calming sense of joy in its stead
It is a metallic steed
That will carry me into the horizon
Lands unknown
And dreams unseen
I am outgrowing the nest
My wings guided by rails
Pistons of my past, passion, hope and faith
Propel me forward
The fuel is all of my decayed dreams
Fossilized rubbish
Converted to
Anthracite

Behold the moment
The only true present
Spoil it not with yesterday's burdens
Nor run from it with tomorrow's fantasies
Be here now
In the suffering or joy
Chaos or peace
Passion or apathy
The solution rests not on distant shores
It is here in this instant
The only change we can make is in this instant
With applied action currently
You can alter the course of your life
Which direction do you choose?
Treading water
Struggling against life's flow
Or do you dare to follow the waterfall
To the bottom shrouded in mist
Will you be ravaged by rocks
Or dive into a pool
What lies past the plunge?
It matters not, first you must commit.
Now!
Behold the moment
The only true present

Ten thousand desired tongues
Playfully worshipping your body
Any sexual fantasy achieved
At what cost though?
Your family destroyed
Your friends cast aside
Exposure to illness
The addiction of desire
Lust is a fix to an addict
Almost as soon as the craving is addressed
It is reestablished
Once you achieve the object of your lust
How long before you set your sights on another?
How long before your fetish wears out
Only to send you deeper into oddity
How complex will your issue become?
Lust will destroy you in trying to keep up
Love is simple
It just is.

A spark to a wick
A candle burning at midnight
An arctic abyss outside
Shrouded in eternal nightfall of Erebus
The combustion of fragrance
Carrying my prayers and intentions
On its scented smoke
My altar illuminated
In the warmth of ritual
To feel the presence grow
As I honor the space more thoroughly
Not talking to detached personification
Talking to the totality
To which I am but a fraction
Knowing that I am as much God
As a cell is a representation of me
Each fragment may contain the whole
But when the whole is limitless
It cannot be contained within one

The moment you realize
You are the catalyst for your dreams
You are closer to them
It's not going to be some grand handed opportunity
It's the endless hours of effort
The recombustion of that initial fire
Late nights, early mornings
Long hours and that extra minute
Wanting to quit but carrying on
Living life like you already achieved it
Constant failures that lead to brief success
Thoroughly accepting you may fail
And instilling vigilance to avoid this
You have to look at reality with dreams
But temper your dreams with reality
I can put the labor into countless things
But if I don't put the labor into sharing it
Will it ever be seen?
The universe can conspire in your favor
Only when you aide it in doing so
The opportunities you are presented with
Aren't magical or fate
They are the byproduct
Of all the energy you have expressed

The current of life
Leading to a precipice
The raging flow
Propelling you
Towards the edge
Clinging to cusp
You survey the abyss below
Shrouded in mist
Concealed by the fog
All that is hidden
Lurks beneath the layers
The options available
Are exhaust yourself grasping
Or embrace the unknown
Diving deep into the depths of faith
You release your fear
And become the flow of the moment
I thought I had picked the path of least resistance
A false assumption blind to reality
Swimming against the current of life
Exhausted and broken on rocks
From surges in the stream
I admitted defeat
Resting in the eddies of life
Outside of the stream of existence
After becoming stagnant
Engulfed in algae I decided to escape
I portaged to a stream
Already flowing the way I wanted to go
I only had to sacrifice
All the unnecessary trappings

That deep down longing
For bare skin on skin
Not just any contact
But that of a lover
A co-conspirator of dreams
To smell
The sweet smell of your skin
And feel the softness of breath
Stroking your hair
Or the curve of your face
Becoming lost
In your beautiful eyes
The radiating warmth
Of your body under the covers
The gentle touch
That makes the storms subside
The sound of your laughter
Echoing in my soul
The flash of your smile
Igniting a thousand suns

My romance is a Xerox
Facsimiles of the last love interest
Bleed into my now
Downloading behaviors I hated
Maybe unconsciously trying to accept you
Maybe just revenge on the innocent
To say that I don't know
Is to ignore reality
To say it doesn't feel wrong
Is to ignore my heart and soul
To say I know how to stop it
Is the lie
Maybe the solution is the end of searching
Maybe it's the beginning of waiting
For the universe to provide
I don't want to damage another
I can bear the pain
I can't bear the pain of inflicting it

It's a certain kind of hell
Being a romantic in the hookup era
An amalgam law of Moore and Murphy
Being mesmerized by minutia
The shimmer of sunlight reflected
Through her left eye while wearing
Crème de la crème
The torture of looking for forever
But finding only fathomless phanstasmic flings
A ceaseless trail of needing more than
Laughter on the cellphone receiver
More connected than ever
But lost in oceans of emotional detachment
I have loved myself back together
Now I am the whipping boy
For the lack of self-love in this century
Your perfume mixed with cigarette smoke
Rests between me and a sense of peace
All I have is trace elements of you
So I place on my mask, a smile
To say you were here, you touched my soul
Now I am here, searching for ghosts

Recreating History

These poems are from the fall of 2017 till the end of
January 2018. They represent an attempt to embrace the
form I used at the beginning of this book. The last four
poems felt like they needed to be included and were
written specifically for the end of the book.

October 2017 - January 2018

The taste of ash
Memories of madness
I have burned
To the point of abandon

The tears of time
Trickle down from heaven
Falling softly
On the faces of the forgotten

Stars in the abyss
Fireflies in pitch
Smell of autumn morn
Sounds of stillness

A galaxy of city lights
Decorate downtown
Shooting star traffic
Police orbit the blocks

The hell of night
Alone and bedded in isolation
The echo of emptiness
The echo of silence

A paint brush of emotion
Colors bleed onto black
Stones, the bones of the earth
Painting with Mardi Gras

A thousand shades
The suffering in silence
Tears have turned to dust
Invisible ink for blood

                                    For me
                          To love is to ache
                         Lost in your face
                Crushed by space. Silence

Autumn mist
Morning rain on leaves
The creek swells
Sounds of water and cricket songs

                          I sprinkled tobacco
                   At the base of the world tree
                       An offering to the spirits
                     A prayer for our ancestors

The taste of loneliness
Yesterday's cold coffee
Stale cigarettes
Mildew hunger mouth

                          Morning mist clings
                    A soft blanket on the day
                            Warm dry socks
                          And vibrant paint

The day birthed
With raindrops on windows
Early morning silence
Alone but not lonely

                    The humid October morning
                       Of an Indian summer
                      The mania of maenads
                    Carried over to autumn

That crunch of
Cool autumn leaves
Creek babbles
On crisp mornings

That cold feeling
Of breaking your own heart
For the millionth time
Just for familiarity

Your words cut
A thousand wounds
On the scar tissue
Of my healing soul

That feeling
Of a dead phone
Not ringing
You swimming in the world

You told me
Shooting stars are common
How?
It's the only one of its make

The brisk light
Of a clear pre-dawn sky
Embraced by action
Intent on inner stillness

That feeling
Of letting go
Not in anger or sadness
But in self-preservation

The cool blue
Piercing through orange fire
Shades of pink clouds
Autumn sunrise

The romantic idealist is dead
Not Because of pain
But because he was exposed
A cruel tyrant of hearts

To be in a relationship
With self
To make love
Within your own soul

Drinking from your loins
To taste the essence of your anatomy
Your yoni longing for my lingam
Sacred sex in written words

To touch your breast
Your breath bursts
My heart races
Your loins flood

Seeking heavens reward
Is a path to hell
Create heaven with kindness
The reward is inherent in the action

Living a prayer
Is gratitude
On every inhale, exhale
And pause

Brush to stone
Color on black
Incense in the air
Body tingling with life

Autumn blooming to winter
Cold embraces the world
A stillness falls outside
The night is silent

                              That silence
                       Intimacy with space
                          A chance for us
                     To explore ourselves

The hush of now
Sounds of the road
The hum of the dishwasher
Silence behind both

                           To accept now
                          For what it is
               Messages with no response
               Conversations with silence

To continue to reach out
To an unresponsive lover
A conversation with an echo
Dating space and silence

                  Tender tendrils of fragrance
                              Fill the void
                     Created by the familiar
                  The tranquility of incense

We become so obsessed
With avoiding death, we forget to live
So adverse to pain
That we fear pleasure

The illumination of now
The stillness in chaos
The constant in change
The message in silence

To love one as oneself
Not for reward or destination
Simply letting the heart free
Not a prisoner or a guard

Connection through space
Quantum entanglement
Two hearts beating
Intertwined by energy

Kundalini coursing through chakras
A cycle of energetic flow
The heart flowing in all
When not blocked by fear

Conventionality dissipates
On the brink of the unknown
The endless horizon
A smile, snarl, laugh

A mind absent
Of criticism
Frees up
Ample energy

I've fallen in love
With too many souls
I've fallen in love
With too few earth women

Anger is a primal emotion
Raw and energetically potent
It creates chasms
An emptiness in aura

Clear away debris
The accumulation of years
In your mind
To see the magic of youth

An altar in my office
Doing the work of the mysteries
A techno shaman
Unraveling reality

In order to move forward
Into any type of meaning
One must be brave
Change takes courage

Expecting the unexpected
The largest expectation
Forget the word expectation
See what is

Spring rain in winter
April in January
Coffee under awning
Listening to nature's concert

Witnessing peace
In this exact moment
Peace is always present
When we look for it

The stillness
Of a winter morning
The silence
Of snowfall

Calm composure
Despite inner anxiety
A still surface
Despite undertow

Melting ice
Warm rain
Thick fog
Early coffee

Wrote a letter
Then slept on it
Don't mail it
Burn it!!

That feeling
Familiar disconnection
Finally realizing
It's not you, it's them

A morning ritual
A center point
To build the rest of your day
Lay your foundation

Do you live with fear of failure
Breathing down your neck
Causing your hairs to stand rigid
Your heart to race
Your mind in flight
Your actions paralyzed
Understand it doesn't matter how many times you fail
Stop worrying about achieving success
In relationships, in careers, in your passions
Use all your failures as bread crumbs
So that when you get somewhere you never imagined
You can look back to who you were at various stages
Make friends with your failures
They will be your greatest teachers
They will be your constant companion
They will be your gateway to success
Success is a byproduct of failure not the opposite of

There is liberation in not getting
Something you have been searching for
Not the liberation that west is fond of espousing
Rather a metaphysical liberation similar to what they seek
Elsewhere
A deeper more meaningful and permanent liberation
That is not dependent upon circumstances
And can thrive despite physical restriction
This liberation is not made for the faint of heart
And may possibly be unattainable intentionally
In my experience when you grasp for it
It slips from your fingers
When you acknowledge you have it
It slides out the window
When you mention it
It remains elusive
The more you think you know about it
The less it shows your understanding of it
It can only be touched
When it wants
And then it is gone

A poem for my future lover

You have sheltered me on sleepless lonely nights
Offered me peace of mind when I could find none
I have spent countless hours heartbroken in your absence
Maybe as many if not more wondering what it will be like?
When we finally meet
To know that out there is a lady who will love me for me
Willing to grow together and through difficulties
That we will share joys grander than imagined
And weather sorrows as a whole
To know that there is a woman willing to teach me
As much as she is willing to learn from me
Able guide me into exploring parts of my personality I didn't know
As much as I am able to do the same for her
To know that this Woman doesn't need completed by my presence
She is a whole as an individual
And that she values the same qualities in me
We may have never yet met
But I feel you out there
Both of us easing into the fact
That the universe will introduce us
When it finds us ready to do so
That no amount of searching
Or effort to find one another
Could ever accomplish any progress
Towards the inevitable first encounter
Our first meeting or our initial interaction
May not even seem that cosmic
The universal trickster
Might make us annoyed by one another's existence
Finding the other to be a hack
Not because of our differences
But because of our similarities
Expressed differently
Maybe this is all part of your plan.
It seems to me that you are trying to trap me
As if I am some shambling beast
Maybe you are right
Maybe I need to step into your web
So I can't escape you
I'd like that

As this book draws to a close
And your eyes gaze the open road
Know that you hold the key
To unlock your destiny
It's never sought only found
When all else seems tumbling down
In the depth of your darkest despair
The brightest light burns steady there
In the pits of your paralyzing fear
Rests your purpose journey there
Find your faith in spirit and self
These connections are true wealth
With light in darkness purpose in fear
Faith in All
You can see clear
An invisible bridge
From here to your dreams
Worry not
About ways or means
Take the steps
Take the leap
Fail or succeed
You must repeat

Thank you for Reading Vagrant Verses

-Ross Cessna January 31, 2018
On the Eve of the Super Blue Blood Moon Lunar Eclipse

www.ingramcontent.com/pod-product-compliance
Lightning Source LLC
Chambersburg PA
CBHW071446090426
42737CB00011B/1798